M000201927

CRYING OUT FOR VINDICATION

THE GOSPEL ACCORDING TO
JOB

DAVID R. JACKSON

P&R
PUBLISHING
P.O. BOX 817 • PHILLIPSBURG • NEW JERSEY 08865-0817

Scripture taken from the HOLY BIBLE: NEW INTERNATIONAL VERSION®. NIV®. Copyright © 1973, 1978, 1984 by International Bible Society. Used by permission of Zondervan.

The "NIV" and "New International Version" trademarks are registered in the United States Patent and Trademark Office by International Bible Society.

Scripture quotations in the appendixes are from the NEW AMERICAN STANDARD BIBLE®. Copyright © 1960, 1962, 1963, 1968, 1971, 1972, 1973, 1975, 1977, 1995 by The Lockman Foundation. Used by permission.

Italics within Scripture indicate emphasis added.

Page design by Tobias Design

Printed in the United States of America

Library of Congress Cataloging-in-Publication Data

Jackson, David R., 1951-
    Crying out for vindication : the Gospel according to Job / David R. Jackson.
        p. cm. — (The Gospel according to the Old Testament)
    Includes bibliographical references and index.
    ISBN-13: 978-1-59638-025-7 (pbk.)
    ISBN-10: 1-59638-025-X (pbk.)
    1. Job (Biblical figure) 2. Bible. O.T. Job—Criticism, interpretation, etc. 3. Bible. O.T. Job—Relation to the New Testament. 4. Bible. N.T.—Relation to Job. I. Title.
    BS580.J5J33 2007
    223'.106—dc22
                                                        2006101517

Dedicated to the memory of the saints who were martyred at Eichenfeld, Ukraine, between 1919 and 1920, and to those who inherited the blessings of their faith and faithfulness, including my mother-in-law, Verna Schroeder; my wife, Patricia; our children and grandchildren; and to all the saints who faithfully maintain their testimony to Christ before the beast today so that others may have the opportunity to hear the gospel and be saved.

CONTENTS

FOREWORD

Concerning this salvation, the prophets, who spoke of the grace that was to come to you, searched intently and with the greatest care, trying to find out the time and circumstances to which the Spirit of Christ in them was pointing when he predicted the sufferings of Christ and the glories that would follow. It was revealed to them that they were not serving themselves but you, when they spoke of the things that have now been told you by those who have preached the gospel to you by the Holy Spirit sent from heaven. Even angels long to look into these things. (1 Peter 1:10–12)

"In addition, some of our women amazed us. They went to the tomb early this morning but didn't find his body. They came and told us that they had seen a vision of angels, who said he was alive. Then some of our companions went to the tomb and found it just as the women had said, but him they did not see." He said to them, "How foolish you are, and how slow of heart to believe all that the prophets have spoken! Did not the Christ have to suffer these things and then enter his glory?" And beginning

with Moses and all the Prophets, he explained to
them what was said in all the Scriptures concerning
himself. (Luke 24:22–27)

The prophets searched. Angels longed to see. And
the disciples didn't understand. But Moses, the prophets,
and all the Old Testament Scriptures had spoken about
it—that Jesus would come, suffer, and then be glori-
fied. God began to tell a story in the Old Testament, the
ending of which the audience eagerly anticipated. But
the Old Testament audience was left hanging. The plot
was laid out, but the climax was delayed. The unfin-
ished story begged an ending. In Christ, God has pro-
vided the climax to the Old Testament story. Jesus did
not arrive unannounced; his coming was declared in
advance in the Old Testament, not just in explicit prophecies of the Messiah but also by means of the stories of
all of the events, characters, and circumstances in the
Old Testament. God was telling a larger, overarching,
unified story. From the account of creation in Genesis
to the final stories of the return from exile, God progressively unfolded his plan of salvation. And the Old
Testament account of that plan always pointed in some
way to Christ.

AIMS OF THIS SERIES

The Gospel According to the Old Testament Series
is committed to the proposition that the Bible, both
Old and New Testaments, is a unified revelation of
God, and that its thematic unity is found in Christ. The
individual books of the Old Testament exhibit diverse
genres, styles, and individual theologies, but tying
them all together is the constant foreshadowing of,
and pointing forward to, Christ. Believing in the fun-
damentally Christocentric nature of the Old Testament,

x

as well as the New Testament, we offer this series of studies in the Old Testament with the following aims:

- to lay out the pervasiveness of the revelation of Christ in the Old Testament
- to promote a Christ-centered reading of the Old Testament
- to encourage Christ-centered preaching and teaching from the Old Testament

To this end, the volumes in this series are written for pastors and laypeople, not scholars.

While such a series could take a number of different shapes, we have decided, in most cases, to focus individual volumes on Old Testament figures—people—rather than books or themes. Some books, of course, will receive major attention in connection with their authors or main characters (e.g., Daniel or Isaiah). Also, certain themes will be emphasized in connection with particular figures.

It is our hope and prayer that this series will revive interest in and study of the Old Testament as readers recognize that the Old Testament points forward to Jesus Christ.

TREMPER LONGMAN III
J. ALAN GROVES

IN MEMORY OF
J. ALAN GROVES

After the death of Ray Dillard in 1993, Al Groves and I saw to the publication of our beloved friend, mentor, and colleague's book, *Faith in the Face of Apostasy*, and in doing so launched a new series. This series, The Gospel According to the Old Testament, aims to show, as Christ himself declared, that "all the Scriptures" speak of our Lord's suffering and glorification (Luke 24:27).

It is with sadness that I report that Al Groves recently died at the age of fifty-four. The sadness of our loss is tempered by the joy we feel that he is now with the Lord he loved and served so well in this life. We owe Al for his insightful teaching, his incisive writing, his work on the Hebrew text for computer use, and, for those of us who knew him, his friendship and encouragement.

TREMPER LONGMAN III

ACKNOWLEDGMENTS

It is appropriate when reflecting on a work such as this to recall those who have had a significant input into one's thinking and understanding. Usually this list includes pastors, academics, and critics—among whom have been the late Alan Begbie, George Robinson, Reg Piper, Terry Dean, Don MacPhail, Greg Fox, Noel Weeks, the late Ray Dillard, the staff and students at William Carey Christian School, and in particular my year 12 classes. A special thank-you is due to the series editor, Tremper Longman III, for his encouragement and helpful criticisms.

I would also like to thank and acknowledge some people whose input has come in another form. Without invading their privacy or wishing to embarrass them, it is appropriate to speak of those whose examples of persevering faith have put flesh on so many aspects of the gospel according to Job.

In the first place, I would like to thank my wife, Patricia, who has constantly brought grace, encouragement, comfort, and wisdom when this man has needed it, often when she herself was most in need.

Second, I have been blessed to know a lady who would, at first glance, appear to be a frail and somewhat timid believer. Some, in passing, might see in her only weakness. To those who have known her, even from childhood, she has been a model of courage in the face of fear, patience through adversity, faith through fire, and always a model of gentleness, meekness, kindness, and generosity that has proven surprisingly powerful. As such I thank God for my mother, Violet Jackson, better known as Pidge, for her love, wisdom, and example.

Significant aspects of the lessons of Job have been made so much more accessible for me through the wisdom and fellowship of Warwick and Ruth Wilkie, John Goldsmith, and Jan Waterhouse, colleagues at William Carey Christian School. I offer them my heartfelt thanks.

With these are a cloud of witnesses, many easily missed, not found among the stars on stage or in public view, but who continue to overcome by faith and who, each week, take their place in the assembly of the saints.

It is a humbling thing to take one's place in such company—it can only be by the grace of Christ.

INTRODUCTION

On a garbage heap, in pain, in desperate mourning for the loss of his children, in poverty, under accusation of friends and provocation of his wife, in an intensity of human emotions that scandalized his pious friends, a man spoke boldly to God and asked "Why?"

At some point in our lives we too have been on that garbage heap and howled to the Lord our "why." It may not be about us but about those closest to us. Sometimes we can see our suffering fitting into a pattern of God's plans and purposes—when it results from persecution or is a direct consequence of our own sin. But at other times it seems random and without purpose—even just plain cruel. At such times we feel ambushed. It is as if an enemy has jumped out of the trees and attacked us.

I discovered Job when I was sitting by my wife's hospital bed, waiting for her to wake up after a miscarriage. We had prayed for this child's safety and salvation since before the child was conceived. We had prayed all that night that the child would survive the present crisis. The answer was no. I sat there, looking out the window of the hospital at sunrise, and watched a bird fly across a cloudless sky as the sun rose. I asked the Lord, "How come that wretched bird could soar through such a sunrise, and our child, made in your image, never see the light of day?" I opened my Bible to Job because I figured he might have something to say at a time like this, and flipped through the pages to roughly the end of the book. I was looking for God's final speech to Job. My eye fell

1

on the questions, "Where were you when I laid the earth's foundations? . . . Have you ever given orders to the morning, or shown the dawn its place? . . . Do you know when the mountain goats give birth? . . . Does the hawk take flight by your wisdom . . . ?" I sat and wept and remembered Job's words, "Naked I came from my mother's womb, and naked I will depart. The LORD gave and the LORD has taken away; may the name of the LORD be praised."

Knowing the Lord at such times is desperately important. Knowing that a sinful response will only increase the pain keeps us from losing perspective. But understanding and being at peace with God at such times is a much bigger issue altogether.

Certainly a good knowledge of God's Word at such times is essential. When the fire of emotions is at its hottest—when the ambush happens—it's too late to want to know. That's the time when we most need to draw on knowledge of the truth that is stored away. It is also a time that creates a hunger to know and understand more.

At such a time I turned to the study of Job, and I invite you to do the same, because through Job we come to Christ. In Jesus our questions and confusions are resolved, our faith vindicated, and our suffering redeemed.

CHAPTER ONE

READING JOB

The book of Job is different in form and style from any other book of the Bible. It is one of those books that you have to be in the mood to read. Many people check it out and put it aside. For those who take the time and get into the issues, reading it is an amazing experience. Somebody once asked my son what his favorite book of the Bible was. I think he was in his early teens at the time. The look on the questioner's face when he said "Job" was worthy of the front cover of any photography magazine. Have you ever met a twelve-year-old who thought Job was the most interesting book of the Bible? He was seven years old when I preached a series on Job in our church. We had lots of fun getting various people in the congregation to read parts as we presented the book of Job as a serialized radio play each week. What made it live was the fact that some harsh things were happening to people in our church at that time, and the book of Job spoke to us of Christ and his part in our struggles. My son didn't know all of the stories then—but the Word of God did come to life as we studied and listened and prayed together. So let's take a moment and think about how we are going to approach this part of God's Word.

No one knows who wrote this book or when, and that is not our primary concern in this study. But it is interesting and worth thinking about if it helps us picture accurately what happened. The book of Job isn't an ancient myth or a timeless story set in never-never land. Myths are about people or creatures who are not located in any identified place or time and are stories that could never be verified. The book of Job is about real people, identified by family name and location, in a real place at a particular time—and so are we.

LISTENING TO JOB AS DRAMA

The book of Job appears to be written in the form of a drama. We have little idea about how this book would have been read or presented in the community where it first appeared. We do know that it would have been read aloud to an audience, since books were copied by hand and were far too expensive for most people to have direct access to a copy.

We know almost nothing about drama, or even if there was something akin to what we call drama or the theater in the ancient Near East.[1] Probably there wasn't. But Job does appear to be written as if a narrator were telling a story and people were reading their parts.

We might imagine the book being presented to an audience much in the way a radio play was presented back in the twentieth century. Even if all the parts were read by one person, there remains an element of drama in the cycle of speeches. Most likely it was presented by a professional reader or storyteller similar to people who ply their trade in many nations today.

The book of Job would be different from what we know as theater because there is no action. The drama is found in the ideas, passion, and logic of the arguments. The audience is drawn into the issues, as into a whirlpool, as the reader gives expression to the frustration and agony reflected in Job's situation and the various ways of trying to make sense of it all.

The hook that draws the audience in is the fact that we all suffer, and from time to time we all see examples of suffering that we think are undeserved, random, or even cruel. All of us struggle with (or try not to think about) the hard questions.

The arguments presented aren't abstract issues. It is about me. It is about the loss of my child. It is about the family I know with two autistic kids. It is about a husband caring for a wife with leukemia. It is about the God who rules a world where a righteous man, a kind and godly man, is murdered. And we all want to know why. Some people want to accuse God, and others want to defend him, but we don't know why he would allow such things to happen. And it hurts.

So we want to jump out of our seats and argue with these men. Like film critics or talk-back radio, we can't just sit and be entertained by this reading of the script. We want to have our say too. And sometimes, when it is all too close to the bone, we want to run away.

The people who heard this drama for the first time would have found it shocking. Job's passion is undignified and confrontational. The friends become so angry they can't even speak. There is a young man who makes a fool of himself by providing the audience with sudden comic relief after all the tension of the argument, just in time to prepare them for the Lord to speak.

Things are said that seem not only to go against the religious beliefs and gods of the local culture, but even to ridicule their claims. As a dramatic reading, Job would invite a pagan culture to rethink everything and challenge its worldview at every point.

In the book of Job we come across references to figures we now know are mythical characters or pagan gods, and who held great significance in the beliefs and customs of a range of people in the ancient Near East. We hear about Mot (Death), Behemoth, Leviathan, and the stars that sing when God lays the foundations of creation. Various speakers allude to ancient myths about Yam (the Sea), Tannin, and Rahab the sea monsters. There is considerable use of poetic imagery drawn from various understandings of the place of the dead. Much of this is difficult to understand because we have an inadequate knowledge of the various forms and developments of these myths in the different communities that passed them down over hundreds of years. What is clear is that Job and his friends are working out the truth in the face of some fearful myths. In that context, Job and others are determined to present God as much more powerful than, more transcendent than, and completely in control of the objects that their contemporaries held in fear and reverence. It is like saying that our God is greater than Superman, Alien, Predator, Godzilla, or Rambo.[2]

This is evangelistic theater and theologizing with a passion. Arguments begun in the public reading of the book of Job have continued up to our time.

In this swirl of passion and ideas, beliefs and fears, Job dug in his heels and fingernails and would not let go of what he knew of "the words of the Holy One," which were God's promises and declaration that he, Job, was righteous.

In this furnace of suffering and confusion, Job's understanding was stretched, and what he knew led him to discover things he didn't understand.

So, let's find out some more about this extraordinary man.

THE SETTING

It is possible that this is the first book of the Bible to have been written. Certainly the events described in this book occurred before any book of the Bible had been written. Immediately we are intrigued. We have the full text of the Word of God in Scripture—for Job, there are no more books to come. This man Job had none of them, so on what basis and with what resources did he manage to go through such experiences without sin (Job 42:7–8)?

The saga of Job is probably set in the period between Abraham and Moses, although it could even be pre-Abrahamic. We know that Job lived in "the east" (Job 1:3), which refers to the land east of the Jordan River. It could be anywhere from Edom (Judg. 6:3) to northern Syria (Haran, the home of Laban; Gen. 29:1). He came from the land of Uz, and a young man who engages in this dispute, Elihu, was a Buzite.

We know of two men named Uz. The first was a son of Aram (Gen. 10:23). The line of covenant succession does not include Aram but follows the line through his brother Arpachshad (Gen. 10:22, 24; 11:11–13). The second man named Uz had a brother named Buz, and these men were Abraham's nephews (Gen. 22:21), sons of his brother Nahor. Nahor's homeland is called Aram-Naharaim. Nahor's son Bethuel was the father of Laban and Rebekah and grandfather of Leah and Rachel. Uz and Buz were Bethuel's brothers. Both Bethuel and Laban are called "the Aramean" (Gen. 25:20; 31:20). It seems as if names such as Aramean or Buzite could be used to identify a man either because he was descended from the one who bore that name originally or because he came from the land once owned by the family of that name. We often find that more than one person will bear the same name. Thus Uz and Buz have a nephew named Aram. While it is possible that Job lived before Abraham, the correlation of the two names, Uz and Buz, lends some probability to a time between Abraham and Moses.

By the sixth century BC, it looks as if the descendants of Uz and Buz may have moved south, into the land of Edom. Jeremiah refers to "the kings of Uz" (Jer. 25:20) in company with the Philistines, Edom, Moab, and Ammon, and the people of Buz (Jer. 25:21–23) in company with

Dedan and Tema in northwestern Arabia. Lamentations locates the Edomites in the land of Uz (Lam. 4:21). In Job 1:15, 17, the raiders who stole his flocks and herds and killed his servants were Sabeans (Arabs) and Chaldeans. The Chaldeans were a people originally associated with the Arameans but who eventually migrated into southern Mesopotamia. If the land of Uz were somewhere near or within the area known as Aram, the distribution of herds and flocks would seem quite logical. Each of these peoples attacked Job's herds and flocks separately. So it is probable that some of Job's flocks and herds may have headed off seeking the pastures south from Aram, along the eastern side of the Jordan, while others went southeast along the Euphrates Valley. It is more difficult to picture them all heading north from a location in Edom and extending along a line of such distance.

In either case we can be reasonably sure that if Job came from the land of Uz, he was descended from Abraham's nephew of that name and that his homeland could have been located anywhere from Aram (northern Syria) to Edom.

Job's children lived in houses, not tents, one of which, when hit by a "mighty wind," fell on his children and killed them (Job 1:19). He was therefore not a nomad, so he and his family would have had to live close to a permanent source of fresh water. His ownership of the land would have involved inheritance and possibly further purchases. He was involved in the breeding of herds of sheep, camels, oxen, and donkeys (1:3), which would require large areas of pasture land and servants who would move with the herds and flocks from one pasture to another, possibly covering significant distances over territory not owned by anyone in particular, making them more vulnerable to raiding parties.

IN THE PINK ZONE

This places Job outside the line of the Abrahamic covenant community. The Bible traces the line of promise from Noah to Jesus, noting along the way that God cut off various branches of this family tree (Ham and Japheth, Ishmael, Esau, and eventually the tribes associated with Joseph) to leave Abraham to Isaac to Jacob to Judah to David and eventually to Jesus. It has been common, on some genealogical charts used for classroom instruction, to trace this line in red. So some Bible teachers speak of the red line that traces the gospel promise from Genesis 3:15 to Jesus.

On such a chart we could say that Job is located in the pink zone. He would be off to the side along with Bethuel, Laban, and Lot.

Throughout the Old Testament, we are repeatedly presented with examples of God's grace to people who lie close to the direct line of God's covenant promises but who are not in that line. Sometimes we are hard-pressed to know this is a matter of kindness or in some instances we might be dealing with saving grace. We can think of people such as Lot (Gen. 19), God's grace to Hagar and Ishmael (Gen. 16:1–16), Laban and his daughters (Gen. 22–35), and later figures such as Ruth, who was a descendant of Lot. Moses' father-in-law was a "priest of Midian" (Ex. 3:1) and seemed to be well accepted within the fellowship of Israel (Ex. 18). God warned Moses and the Israelites not to "abhor" the Edomites because they were "your brothers" (Deut. 2:8–9; 23:7; cf. Num. 20:21). David sent his family to safety in the care of the king of Moab (1 Sam. 22:3).

And so, while the line of promise may point us to Christ, those adjacent to that line seem also to have come within the pale of God's grace in various ways. Who knows but how many of them will be found among the company

9

of God's faithful people on that day. What is clear is that there is grace, even saving grace, to some who were born in the pink zone, and Job would be one such.

JOB'S PLACE IN HISTORY

We can fairly conclude that Job lived between the time of Abraham and Moses. We draw this conclusion based on several indications in the text.

First, there is no mention in the book of the name or nation of Israel.

Second, in Job's day there was no centralized sacrificial system based within the nation of Israel, located at the one tabernacle or temple and serviced by priests descended from Aaron. Rather, we find the same practices that we see in Genesis, where the patriarch, as head of his family, acted as priest by offering sacrifices and praying for his household (Job 1:5). Like the patriarchs, Job could pray for people other than his family (Job 42:8–9; cf. Gen. 20:17).

Third, Job's lifespan must have been around 200 years. He lived long enough to marry and raise a family of adult children who had in turn all been married and then killed. Then he lived another 140 years (Job 42:16). As such, Job's lifespan is longer than that of Moses and the generations after him and is more in keeping with those of the patriarchs closer to Abraham's day. According to Genesis 10, the lifespan of people after the flood dropped quickly. Between Shem and Peleg, people lived for something just over 400 years. With Peleg, the age span dropped suddenly to less than 250, and as we move from Abraham to Joseph, the drop continued steadily. So Abraham's grandfather Nahor lived for 148 years; his father, Terah, 205; then Abraham died at 175 (Gen. 25:7), Isaac at 180 (Gen. 17:1), Jacob at 130 (Gen. 47:9), Joseph at 110, and

Moses at 120. Job's lifespan thus would place him earlier rather than later in the patriarchal period.

Fourth, apart from the book of Job, the name Job occurs in the Old Testament only in Ezekiel 14:14, 20, where Ezekiel refers to the biblical Job. Outside the Bible, however, the name occurs in a nineteenth-century BC Egyptian curse on a Palestinian clan chief; on an eighteenth-century Egyptian list of slaves, some of whom bear Semitic names; on eighteenth-century tablets from Alalakh and sixteenth-century tablets found at Mari; in the fourteenth-century Amarna letters; and in the thirteenth-century Ugaritic texts.[3] So, we can be fairly sure that Job lived some time between 2000 and 1400 BC.

AND OURS

We live at a time when more Christians are being persecuted and killed for the sake of the gospel than at any other time in history. There are so many Jobs on ash heaps in more countries than ever before. And in various ways, all who put their faith in Christ will have to deal with the same issues and challenges.

Here we discover, with Job, more of the depth of God's grace to us in Christ—who, by his own choice, suffered more than Job to save us from the cruelty and domination of sin. At the worst of times, when we are ambushed and wounded, we need to know, to believe, and to cling to these things. And so we join the audience and come to learn the wisdom of the gospel according to Job.

FOR FURTHER REFLECTION

1. What are some of your "why" questions that you would like God to answer?

11

2. What aspects of the gospel do you find difficult or confusing?

3. Apart from life itself, what is so valuable to you that its loss would have the possibility of breaking your grip on Christ and the gospel? Where is your faith vulnerable?

PART ONE

A TIME TO CRY OUT

CHAPTER TWO

THE SCENE IN HEAVEN (1:6–2:13)

Probably the best window into a generation's thinking is the music or the movies that hit the harmonic for them. The period from about the ages of twelve to twenty-five seems to be the time when so many issues are decided and so much of life is being shaped on the forge. It helps to listen to the music of the next generation and to check out the movies that younger people like, because through them we can pick up "the wind" of the times.

In the late 1970s we had a wave of movies featuring the hero who had to step outside the law to bring justice and protect us all. For the past twenty years, we have been subjected to waves of songs and movies that reflect the idea that we are victims of conspiracy and that we are essentially helpless. In 1986, the heavy-metal group Metallica[1] sang about the "Master of Puppets" who controls your life by getting into your mind and dreams, leaving you blind and screaming.

Since then we have had lots of movies about extraterrestrials or the Central Intelligence Agency or the Vatican (interesting juxtaposition of bad guys, isn't it?) running secret operations to control the world. My favorite scene is the last one in *Men in Black*, when the camera zooms across the solar system and through all the galaxies until it comes out of the universe to find a large, weird-looking creature playing marbles. Our cosmos is one of his marbles.

Is that how it is? Are we little humans scurrying around on planet Earth like so many bugs ("unevolved pond scum," as the bad guy in *Men in Black* put it), living helpless and pointless lives controlled by beings we neither see nor hear? Are we here for the amusement of some out-of-this-world beings who are bored?

Such ideas aren't new. Similar ideas are found in the myths of the Egyptians, Assyrians, Canaanites, Greeks, and Babylonians, having all the dignity of ancient cultures, archaelogical relics, exotic religions, and long-lost texts. For God's people who lived in such cultural settings, these weren't movies. These ideas were the state religion backed by some intimidating people in positions of power.

As Christians who hold to the Bible as God's words of revelation, we are at a bit of a disadvantage when it comes to arguments about such things. We do have the Bible, and we do have a risen Savior who came into the world, died, and came back to talk to us. But we don't have firsthand knowledge of heaven or what goes on there. We don't have a detailed picture of what God is going to do or why he does what he does most days of the week. Speculation can fill that picture quite quickly with some exciting scenarios that sell lots of books. But most of the time we have to admit, "I simply don't know." On any given day, these things probably aren't all that important for us, that is, until life hits the fan and the bits fly everywhere. So our author begins by giving the audience (but not Job) the information we need to make sense of what is about to happen. We are in on the conspiracy, and he is not.

ACT 1, SCENE 1: JOB HOLDS COURT (1:5)

Job's seven sons seem to be enjoying an idyllic family lifestyle. As each one has a birthday (Job 1:4; cf. 3:1, where Job curses "his day" and proceeds to talk about the day he was born), the whole family assembles for a party. These parties seem to last for a week (1:5). Then Job brings everyone together and offers whole burnt offerings to cover their sin, just in case. Here is the head of the family summoning his sons for a series of sacrifices before they return to their homes and labors. Job's court is then a temple scene, a temple being a place where God and humankind meet. Here Job is priest and mediator representing his family before the throne of God.

ACT 1, SCENE 2: GOD HOLDS COURT (1:6–12)

The scene in heaven is set deliberately as a parallel to the scene at Job's house. Here we have God, his sons, and one who appears to be an intruder.

This scene immediately brings us, and possibly the original audience, into some confusion. Who are these people? Throughout the ancient Near East we have a range of different versions of what one might see in the heavenly assembly. Across a number of traditions from Greece to Mesopotamia, one could fairly expect to find an assembly of gods with one god taking supremacy over the rest. Whatever other beings might be found there, it is these gods who determine what happens on earth, and more often than not they are found having all manner of disputes with one another.

There are several places in the Bible where allusion is made to this pagan conception of heaven. Many of these passages are hard to understand, and we need to tread carefully and not attempt to explain away lightly the difficulties. Nevertheless, there are lines that need to be drawn. When the biblical writers call on "the gods" to worship Yahweh (Ps. 97:7), it doesn't mean they are saying that there are many gods in heaven who need to vote for Yahweh and accept him as their leader. The men who translated the Old Testament into Greek before Jesus was born seem to have been troubled by this and other such passages (cf. Ps. 8:5; 138:1), so they translated the Hebrew word for "gods" as "angels." Over time, the practice developed of identifying pagan idols with angels, and then realizing that these must be sinful angels. Where information is lacking, speculation will flow.

There certainly is a "host of heaven" (1 Kings 22:19), including spiritual beings that are not human. There are beings called "angels" and "spirits" (Zech. 6:5) or "watchers/guardians" (Dan. 4:13, 17, 23). It is difficult in some places to say whether the writer is referring to the pagan understanding of what is in heaven or whether he is affirming that this is reality. Even where we are sure the writer is describing reality, it is another thing to be able to sort out whether the creatures in view are all angels. It could be quite a leap to claim that since "sons of God" can appear in Yahweh's court, they must be angels.

One of the things happening in the book of Job is a sophisticated polemic targeting such pagan beliefs.[2] The author of Job makes some heavy use of the mythology and culture of his time to portray Yahweh as the only God, creator, and sovereign over all else in creation. He makes ironic use of mythical figures such as Leviathan and Rahab to portray Yahweh as supreme, especially in Job 38–41. While wishing to be careful not to import pagan concepts into Job's worldview, we need to admit that some passages in Job are particularly difficult to understand, and in such places we do well to postpone our thoughts in hope of greater light.

SONS OF GOD

Amid the pagan conceptions of heaven we find a tradition, well represented in the Ugaritic literature, that represents "sons of the gods" as the spirits of the deceased, also known as "rephaim" (cf. Job 26:5; Prov. 21:16; Isa. 14:9). These spirits are in some way associated with the spirits of the dead kings. Throughout the ancient Near East, kings claimed that their right to rule was based on their relationship with a god or gods. Occasionally we find the claim that they either are gods or become gods when they die. More commonly, they were believed to be the sons of the gods. Against this arrogant and idolatrous boast, the biblical prophets occasionally spoke in terms loaded with sarcasm and judgment. Thus the two passages often understood to be accounts of the origins of Satan, Isaiah 14:3–23 and Ezekiel 28:1–19, are prophecies directed at the hubris of the kings of Babylon and Tyre, respectively, who had made such claims for themselves. King Herod's acceptance of the people's cries that he was a god resulted in his death by worms (Acts 12:20–23) and recalls this prophecy (Isa. 14:11–12).

Who, then, are the "sons of God" in Job?

With only a few possible exceptions (Gen. 6:1–4; Job 1:6; 2:1), throughout the Bible "sons of God" is always a reference to God's believing people—his chosen people. About the third century BC, a Jewish cult arose that saw angels as "sons of God" and taught that they were the main cause of evil on earth. This cult is known today as Enochic Judaism, and it includes the Essenes, or the Dead Sea Scrolls cult. It would have been against this teaching that the writer of the epistle to the Hebrews posed the rhetorical question, "For to which of the angels did God ever say, 'You are my Son; today I have become your Father'? Or again, 'I will be his Father, and he will be my Son'?" (Heb. 1:5). In the forefront of this confrontation is the writer's understanding of the person of Jesus as *the* Son of God. Nevertheless, "the sons of the kingdom" are humans, not angels (Matt. 13:36–43), as are the "holy ones" to whom the kingdom is awarded in Daniel 7:22, 27. From Adam (Luke 3:38) to Israel (Ex. 4:22–23; Hos. 11:1) to David's heir (2 Sam. 7:14), Solomon (1 Chron. 22:9–10), to us (John 1:12; 1 John 3:1), the title refers to humans.

There is no doubt that in Job 38:7 they are mythical beings, synonymous with the stars, who are depicted as singing when the foundations of the earth were laid. Jews who followed the teachings of *1 Enoch* saw problems with this verse. In the Aramaic Targum on Job that was found in their library (11Q10 xxx.5), the stars "shine" rather than "sing," and "the sons of God" are "angels," in keeping with the distinctive way the followers of the Enoch tradition developed their version of the cosmic conspiracy. According to their thinking, angels were in charge of, not identical with, stars, the sun, the moon, and everything that affected the seasons and the calendar. The problem with the picture in Job 38:7, however, is that according to Genesis 1, there were no stars (and presumably then no such "sons of God") when the foundations of the earth were laid, because stars weren't created till day four! Job is here borrowing another picture from pagan mythology as part of his polemic against those who feared the powers in the sky or the sea.

It was a scandalous concept then, as it is in some circles now, to conceive of human beings standing so close to the throne of God in heaven. Those who translated the Old Testament into Greek tended to word their translation so as to put as much distance as possible between God and men. For man to be next in rank under God was shocking, and so the statement in Psalm 8:5 is changed, placing man a little lower than the angels rather than a little lower than God, as the Hebrew text states (cf. Heb. 2:7). The New Testament writers stood their ground on the matter, with Paul firmly declaring that God's people

would "judge angels" (1 Cor. 6:3) and that angels are servants sent by God to serve us (Heb. 1:14) and especially
our covenant head, Jesus.

In a scene reminiscent of this one, the writer to the
Hebrews calls on Christians to be aware of their place
in this heavenly assembly. Yes, the heavenly assembly
includes angels. But it is preeminently an assembly before
the throne of God of "the firstborn, whose names are
written in heaven . . . the spirits of righteous men made
perfect" (Heb. 12:22–24). In the New Covenant church,
the heavenly and earthly temples have merged—we have
already come to Mount Zion.

It is particularly significant then that Job 1:6–12 does
not mention angels. The satan's challenge is in fact not
just a charge against Job, but against all the sons of God
present in that assembly. Job is simply the test case. The
satan is challenging the right of every son of God to stand
before the throne of God.

THE SATAN

Who is this "satan"? Here the picture is very vague,
and possibly deliberately so. None of our questions are
addressed: "Where did he come from?" "What is he doing
in the throne room of God in heaven?" In fact, Satan
isn't even his name here. He is "the satan," a title that
means simply accuser or opponent. Without any explana-
tion, he appears in the way an ancient king's spy might
arrive at court to report on a corrupt official. He func-
tions as a prosecutor and doesn't have a name. To
identify him as Satan or the devil requires further
revelation such as came much later, as in Zechariah
3:1–7. We are not even told that the snake in the garden
of Eden was Satan until Revelation 12:9! It is only
with this benefit of hindsight that we can identify "the
satan" of Job with the one who bears the name

Satan, the devil, or a number of other titles in later revelation. One might fairly conclude that for the author of Job, he isn't that significant a person—or is this a polemical device to treat the enemy with contempt?

What we do know of Satan throughout the Bible helps us make sense of this scene—much more so than the original audience. For the sake of simplicity we shall therefore refer to him as Satan, keeping in mind that we do so with the benefit of the rest of Scripture.

We know that Satan was the one who tempted Eve and Adam. His success in Genesis 3 turned the order of the world upside down. Whereas God was owner and man and woman ruled the world under God (Gen. 1:28), now man and woman had declared independence from God and found themselves under the dominion of an animal. All of humanity thereafter, being born on Adam's side of the war with God, were born enemies of God—until Jesus! In him at last we find another man who enters the world without sin and so is entitled to rule the earth. This man had to face the same challenge, and Satan, to continue in power, had to bring him down.

Immediately following his baptism with water and the Holy Spirit, Jesus went off into what is significantly now wilderness and not garden, to face this enemy one on one. In the course of this encounter, we hear the enemy make this claim and offer:

> The devil led him up to a high place and showed him in an instant all the kingdoms of the world. And he said to him, "I will give you all their authority and splendor, for it has been given to me, and I can give it to anyone I want to." (Luke 4:5–6)

Jesus came to take possession of the kingdom of God. He came to be anointed (Ps. 2), and then enthroned as king in Adam's place (Rom. 5:12–21). He is "the Son of Man" whom Daniel saw, who would ascend to heaven and be enthroned at the right-hand side of "the Ancient of Days" (Dan. 7:13–14; Acts 1:9; 2:33). For him to have a people to rule, he would need to die on a cross to redeem them. In the wilderness temptation, Satan was offering Jesus a way to get the throne without going to the cross. I still delight to recall Les Sloat, our Greek instructor at Westminster Seminary, as he gave such expression to Jesus' blunt reply to Satan in Matthew 4:10, where the Greek word is "Hoopagay": "Get lost!"

Satan was defeated at this encounter. A man had chosen to suffer in order to maintain his faithfulness to God and thus to purchase righteousness for all the children of God! This same being, called "the satan" in Job 1, hopes no man would ever make such a choice. On a smaller scale prophetic of suffering, Job will show us that our Redeemer will make that choice.

We next hear of Satan in the Gospels, when Jesus says as the seventy return (Luke 10:18), "I saw Satan fall like lightning from heaven." We have to wait till Revelation 12 to learn that, having failed to kill the promised child, Satan was thrown out of heaven. John tells us the good news that "the accuser of our brothers, who accuses them before our God day and night, has been hurled down" (Rev. 12:10).

This means that the prosecutor who failed will become the vigilante who would kill. The age of persecution begins, and it is Satan's last desperate attempt to keep the kingdoms of this world for himself (Rev. 12:11–17; Dan. 7:21–22; 24–27; 1 Peter 5:8).

The court case that we first hear about in Job 1–2 ends with Jesus. Now we have been given the right to be called the children of God (John 1:12). We have been vindicated at the cost of his suffering and death. Now we must face the beast in the flesh and suffer and persevere to gain the kingdom of God. And so the call to perseverance and faith rings long and loud through the pages of the New Testament as the authors of those Scriptures began to experience what today is global and intense persecution. Together with those who have already overcome, we await the final encounter with Satan, when the heavenly court shall again convene and Jesus will open the books (Rev. 20:11–15), vindicate us, and bring an end to our suffering.

FOR FURTHER REFLECTION

1. Reflect on the movies and the songs that moved you when you were in your teens. Why did those songs strike such a harmonic with you then? What were the issues, and what answers did they offer? What answers did or will your generation pass on to the next?
2. What better answers from God's Word do you have now to pass on? With whom should you be having such conversations?
3. Are you intimidated when you tell others about the gospel? Why?
4. What do you know about what happens to us when we die? Can you find a basis for these ideas in the Bible, or is there an element of wishful thinking mixed in?
5. How much of what you know or believe about Satan can you find in the Bible?
6. Do you ever "believe" what you "imagine to be true"?

CHAPTER THREE

THE QUESTION (1:6–2:13)

T hings that delight a father's heart: We have four
children now grown to adulthood. If I look back and
recall the things that made my heart soar, probably
the highest points of all were when I found my children
making the right choices when they thought I wasn't looking. The best of kids will make sure that when their Mom
or Dad is around, they do and say things that will make
them happy. But what about when Dad and Mom are not
there? What choices will they make then? What thoughts
will they express? What do they really think (Prov. 20:6)?
Generally it is best if we don't inquire, and they enjoy the
dignity of their privacy (Eccl. 7:21). Still, it is when they
fly solo that we find out what they're made of.

In the book of Judges we learn that God left the people
of Israel to their own consciences after the exodus and
conquest of the land. There was no centralized government
and no police to enforce the law of God. "Everyone did as
he saw fit" (Judg. 21:25). In a land of total liberty the hearts
of God's people were revealed, and it wasn't a happy scene.
Not surprisingly, they quickly asked to give up their liberty
for a king like the nations who would bring law and order.

It is one thing to be faithful when those who enforce
the law are watching. It is another to do it because we want

to. Our state government decided some time ago to set up speed cameras at points where there was a high frequency of road accidents. These cameras record the speed and the license plate of the offender's vehicle and take a photograph of the offense as it happens. They are also placed at traffic lights to photograph vehicles crossing against the red light. It is fascinating to drive through these areas and see the traffic flow drop an average of about 10 miles per hour below the speed limit just so drivers make sure they don't get ticketed! And then they speed up again as soon as they are through the intersection. Radio stations have great fun letting drivers know where the moveable speed traps are. The results are beyond dispute—accidents, injuries, and deaths are cut virtually to zero at these locations. What then if the law were observed by all because we were convinced it was the right thing to do and would save lives? What if we didn't need the cameras and the police and the fines?

Satan knows human sinful nature well. He has plenty of evidence to prove that if left to themselves, people make wrong choices. We know too that what is said and done at church on Sunday doesn't necessarily last till Monday morning. So Satan comes to court with an argument supported by an overwhelming body of evidence—and he hadn't even heard of the period of the judges!

ACT 1, SCENE 2 CONTINUED (1:6–12)

As Satan approaches the throne of God, it is God who initiates the encounter with what appear to be some pretty naïve moves. The audience is familiar with the fact that Yahweh knows and sees all (Prov. 21:2; cf. Jer. 23:24). So why does he ask, "Where have you come from?" This apparent naïveté should really fool only a fool. The question is a move in a chess game, and as such it is a setup. But why the game? It isn't a bet with a prize for the winner.

26

Who will benefit from this encounter? God won't learn anything he doesn't already know. Satan isn't going to change his position, and God knows that too. So who is going to benefit from all this?

The encounter is about two groups of people. The first group is us—the children of God. This whole saga is going to be for our benefit to reveal and teach us something of the gospel. It is only as we participate in this series of events and arguments, albeit as readers of the narrative, that we will come to understand and be able to apply the things God is here setting out to tell us. And these are things that we will need to know if we are to persevere in faith and overcome. This is then a training exercise for all the sons and daughters of God.

The second group to benefit is the audience, not mentioned, but in the heavenly scene, made up of the rest of the heavenly host. The members of the heavenly audience, who are not in need of redemption, will witness God's display of his character and of the gospel and they, with God's people on earth, and eventually those yet to be born, will glorify God. And therein lies the secret to it all.

In a catechism that we developed for our children, we put the question "Why did God make you and everything else?" The answer is "for his own glory" (memory verse, Rev. 4:11). It comes as a shock to people to discover that everything is not for our benefit. In Ezekiel 20, God rebukes a people who thought that being born Jewish somehow put God under obligation to save them. He tells them bluntly why he saved them: "for the sake of my name I did what would keep it from being profaned" (Ezek. 20:9). This point is made seven more times in this chapter in various forms (Ezek. 20:14, 22, 26, 38, 41, 42, 44). God does not commit idolatry and worship us. He is not there for us. Quite the contrary, we are here for him—put here for his glory. Even his enemies are created to glorify him. Having emphasized the grace of God but ignored everything else about God, Christians now face a community of people who are convinced that God, like everyone else, owes us. Ultimately, it isn't about us, but about him and his glory. And our salvation in that context, and only in that context, is grace, not one of our many civil liberties.

It is similarly shocking to find that God will, to make a point, use real people in history. When the New Testament tells us that these things that happened in the Old Testament were "warnings" and "examples" for us (1 Cor. 10:6, 11; Heb. 4:11; James 5:10–11; 2 Peter 2:6; Jude 7) and that they are there to teach us, we need to pause and take in the gravity of that statement. At what cost were these lessons and revelations given to us? How many have had to die for us to learn these things? God means it when he says, through the prophet Isaiah (see Rom. 9:22–24):

> For I am the LORD, your God,
>   the Holy One of Israel, your Savior;
> I give Egypt for your ransom,
>   Cush and Seba in your stead.
> Since you are precious and honored in my sight,
>   and because I love you,
> I will give men in exchange for you,
>   and people in exchange for your life.
>   (Isa. 43:3–4)

As we shall see, this pattern continues to this day as the gospel comes to us through the suffering of many, and goes out still in the same way. And God says it is worth the suffering, because it will bring salvation to many, and it will bring glory to his name.

So with a face to Satan, and as it were, a sly glance to the audience, God begins the encounter (Job 1:7–8) with "Where have you come from?" and moves quickly to initiate a focus on "my servant Job."

Hartley in his commentary, notes,

> Proudly Yahweh called Job *his servant*. . . . The
> greatest leaders in the OT bear the title *servant*, a
> title that indicates God himself acknowledges their
> humble services, which he has commissioned, e.g.
> Abraham (Ps. 105:6, 42), Jacob or Israel (Isa. 41:8),
> Moses (Ex. 14:31), Joshua (Josh. 24:29), David
> (2 Sam. 7:5, 8), Isaiah (Isa. 20:3), and the prophets
> (2 Kings 9:7; Amos 3:7).[1]

What is remarkable about this man, Job, is that he is
"blameless and upright, a man who fears God and shuns
evil" (Job 1:8). God has, as it were, picked his best man to
put forward as the bait because "there is no one on earth
like him."

Yahweh's testimony with respect to Job's standing
before God is fundamental to everything that follows.
Without this, the audience would be left with no option
but to side with Job's friends in thinking him conceited and
self-righteous and so worthy of God's displeasure.

So it was also for those who knew Jesus. Going by all
appearances, he was a Galilean who was arrested, mocked,
tried and found guilty, scourged and crucified, and failed
to get himself down from the cross to defeat his enemies.
He died. For those who took the messianic promises of the
Old Testament seriously, there would be no alternative but
to conclude that he was yet another false Christ.

But God did speak and bear witness concerning Jesus.
Recalling the words of Isaiah 42:1, God's voice is heard
on more than one occasion (Matt. 3:17; cf. 17:5) to say,
"This is my Son, whom I love; with him I am well pleased."
The word for "Son" used in Isaiah 42:1 means something
like our English word "boy" and can refer to a servant or
a son. The Lord's servant, in Isaiah, as he is about to be
in Job, is a suffering servant (Isa. 52:13–53:12). But he is
also "blameless and upright" and has God's approval, and
he is God's boy—his beloved Son.

THE CHALLENGE (1:9–11)

Satan jumps to the bait. He is rightly named "the accuser." His challenge is more an accusation against God than against Job. As Anderson puts it:

> With vulgar manners he refuses to use the conventional courtesies of court etiquette which avoided the personal pronouns by addressing a superior as "my lord" instead of "you" and using the deferential "your slave" instead of "I." The Satan's "thou" is thus insulting. Incidentally, this is further evidence that the Satan does not belong to the circle of God's respectful servants.[2]

Satan is accusing God of lying. "You" have put a hedge around Job. "You" have blessed him and given him everything. This, in response to God's claim that Job is blameless and upright, is a thinly veiled way of saying that Job is no such thing. God can make such claims only by, as it were, bribing Job to be what God wants him to be. So Satan calls on God to put forth "your hand" and take away all Job's blessings and we'll soon see what kind of a man he is. With a sneer of sarcasm, Satan concludes (Job 1:11), "Surely he will bless you to your face." Rightly, translators have long seen in this expression the opposite expectation.[3]

The challenge then is a simple one. Satan is saying that none of God's people love him more than they love themselves. Their love for God, and their faithfulness to him, is not God-centered but self-centered. It's about what they get out of God. He is accusing God of running a nasty protection racket, instead of what God is claiming it to be, a salvation based on grace evoking a personal faith that has integrity.

For the believer, there would appear here to be great danger. For the original audience of the book of Job, there is genuine drama at this point. The history of ancient Near Eastern royal families is strewn with the bodies of royal sons who were denounced to their fathers. The accuser enters the royal court and whispers into the king's ear that his son or wife is plotting against him or that their public declarations of loyalty are nothing more than goods for sale to the highest bidder. The accuser risks his life to make such a claim. If the king be convinced, then heads roll, and often as not the accuser's backers turn out to be the real plotters seeking power. In Jesus' day, the household of King Herod was a hotbed of such plots and accusations. The audience at this point would be aware that on this accusation, everything is at stake—not only is Job's integrity in question, but so much more, God's. If now Job should fail, every believer is deemed a fraud.

The central issue in the book of Job is not the justice of God in allowing an innocent man to suffer, or whether the power of Satan is greater than God's, but the integrity of saving faith and the gospel being believed. Is there such a thing as genuine faith? And if there is, how will it respond when ambushed by calamity? For in the heat of the moment, the true heart is revealed. Surely, if Satan could catch Job by surprise, he would not bless God. No. The instant reaction would be to let fly. Maybe later, when things cool off and emotions settle, we might get a better response, but that will have been rehearsed, and it could be nothing more than an act. To see the real Job, Satan will need to catch him by surprise.

So God sends Satan after the bait, and he is quick to be about his business. We note that he acts under God's rule. There is no dualism here—we are not dealing with two equal opponents competing for a prize. God alone is on the throne, and Satan acts only with God's permission and according to what serves God's purposes. As such, his opposition to God makes him all the more the fool.

ACT 1, SCENE 4: SKIN FOR SKIN (2:1-6)

Like a fool who will not learn, Satan is not easily dis-
couraged. Job's losses and the suddenness and rapidity
with which the news of events is delivered to his door
have failed to bring about Satan's predicted result. Job's
response is a faithful one. So it is back to God's court.

Once again God presents a naïve demeanor to a crafty
opponent. In seeming ignorance he asks again (Job 2:2-3),
"Where have you come from? . . . Have you considered my
servant Job?" It is as if God missed act 1, scene 3, and so
we pass over it and stay with events in God's courtroom.
The audience, however, has missed nothing. God's feigned
ignorance strikes them as having an edge of the triumphant
grin about it. And so it is. Of course God knows, and so he
quickly changes the mood and returns the charge to Satan
(Job 2:3), "And he still maintains his integrity, though you
incited me against him to ruin him without any reason."

Embedded in this reply is a serious charge. God states
that the loss suffered by Job is unjust—it is "without any
reason." The responsibility for that loss is now laid directly
to the account of Satan. He is now liable for what has and
will happen. Had Job cursed God and Satan been proved
correct, things would be different. But if the charge fails,
the accuser bears the responsibility, so Satan now is in
serious trouble. Either he must back down in disgrace
and face the consequences, or he must up the stakes and
go for broke.

Killing Job, however, would not settle the question.
Satan needs a living Job to make the decision as to whether
he will be faithful or not. Satan now calls for everything
else to be put on the table, and God agrees. What is a
man's breaking point? Is there a price a man will not pay
to maintain his faith in the Lord? Surely he will give up
anything to save his own skin.

Once again Satan is quick to be about his business, and
he is able to do so only by order of God. It is interesting that

it is only Satan who crosses from one court to the other. It is also interesting that his departure from the presence of the Lord in Job 2:7 is his exit from the book of Job.

We are left with two questions. First, where then is Satan, and why is he not returning to God's courtroom? This question is quickly answered. He has failed, and he has made a fool of himself. He does not return to face God but has disappeared. We need then to cast our eye throughout the rest of the Bible to see where else he will surface.

But a more intriguing question awaits our attention. Where is Jesus in all of this? Where is our advocate (1 John 2:1)? Where is the defense attorney for Job?

One could proffer several possible answers. Obviously it is God's purpose to settle this matter by actions rather than by legal argument. But there is another reality here. Satan's case is not ultimately thrown out of court until Jesus has defeated him in person as a man. It is after he has come in the flesh and has been anointed with the Holy Spirit as the rightful king, and after *he* faithfully resists Satan's temptations, that this case is settled. God has chosen to become man in order to suffer, including "skin for skin" and death itself, to redeem God's people and to raise up the children of God. It was always God's plan to settle the question by actions rather than argument. And so we read (Acts 2:23, 32–33, 36),

> This man was handed over to you by God's set purpose and foreknowledge; and you, with the help of wicked men, put him to death by nailing him to the cross. . . . God has raised this Jesus to life, and we are all witnesses of the fact. Exalted to the right hand of God, he has received from the Father the promised Holy Spirit and has poured out what you now see and hear. . . . Therefore let all Israel be assured of this: God has made this Jesus, whom you crucified, both Lord and Christ.

Now, our advocate need not argue the case. The case is settled. Now, when the saints are attacked, he simply rises to his feet (Acts 7:55–56), and all of heaven knows that he will not deny any who come to him (John 6:37) but will receive them as his own, and judgment and justice are about to be done. For us, then, the matter is settled at the throne of God, and that is the location of our assurance.

FOR FURTHER REFLECTION

1. When left to yourself, what attitudes or desires come to the surface?
2. Take some time to go back and identify the passages in this section of Job that might offend or put people off.
3. Apart from Jesus, how many people had to suffer and die for you to hear the gospel and have the opportunity to come to Christ?
4. Do you love the Lord because he saved you and gave you an eternal inheritance, or simply because of who he is? Do you love him more than you value the things he gives you in Christ?
5. Take the time to read through the Gospel accounts of Jesus' last week. Stand, as it were, at the foot of the cross, and tell him how you feel.

CHAPTER FOUR

THE RESPONSE: WISDOM

An ambush works because people are predictable. Unless one is trained to the point where one reacts the right way without having to think about it, the victim will do exactly the wrong thing. There is no time in an ambush to stop and think. There certainly is no time to read the manual. And so it is when this satan launches his attack. As he leaves the presence of God, he goes to prepare an ambush that will be devastating in its multiple layers of shock and overwhelming force.

Wisdom is the skill of godly living. It is the product of training in godliness. The Bible compares this to the training of the tradesman (Ex. 31:1-11; cf. 1 Cor. 3:9-10), the master craftsman. The writer of Proverbs noted (22:29), "Do you see a man skilled in his work? He will serve before kings; he will not serve before obscure men." Wisdom is about being able to do things at a high level of sophistication. Whereas knowledge lays the basis for wisdom, wisdom is happening when the knowledge is applied without having to think about it. It is like the difference between merely knowing what to do to drive a car, and actually being able to drive through city traffic without being aware of the process of driving. It has become second nature. Wisdom is knowledge plus practice across a range of experience.

Jesus is presented to us in the New Testament as the personification of wisdom, not only in his innocence but particularly in his ability to handle his enemies. Presented with impossible choices, Jesus turns the tables on his opponents and hangs them on the horns of their own arguments (Matt. 22:15–33; Mark 12:1–12). Those who attempted to ambush Jesus found themselves ambushed, and that publicly. Today, people of interest to the news media have to learn quickly the skills of handling the ambush interview. Every Christian needs those skills.

The speed and smoothness of Jesus' repartee was not just for his amusement. Those who follow him are rightly called "disciples." Today the word "disciple" carries religious connotations. The word we translate as "disciple" was simply an ordinary term for a "student" or an "apprentice." Jesus' disciples were there to learn his skills because he came to end our ignorance and foolishness and give us back the wisdom Adam lost. As we come to the book of Job, we come as apprentices and students of Christ.

Job's responses to Satan's attacks are rightly understood as models of wisdom that point us to Christ. That makes those who oppose him, especially Satan, models of foolishness. As we come then to the scenes on earth, we turn to watch a master of godliness in action and to see something of the skills we need to learn. And so back to Job's court.

ACT 1, SCENE 3: JOB'S HOUSE (1:13–19)

We find Job at his house receiving messengers who bring reports from the various ends of Job's property. Each one comes from a different direction, so that within minutes, he is hit from all sides with the most devastating news. Each announcement is worse than the one before it, reaching a truly awful climax.

The first blow comes from the Sabeans, who took his thousand oxen and five hundred donkeys. We know very little about the Sabeans in the second millennium BC, except that this is one of the terms used to identify the Arab tribes that lived to the south of Edom. It is worth noting that Job's oxen were plowing. His is no nomadic lifestyle, and to have five hundred pairs of oxen available to plow fields indicates some huge land holdings. The slaughter of the servants would similarly be no small massacre.

The next assault comes from heaven. "The fire of God" refers to a lightning strike. Some people have had difficulty with how a lightning strike could kill seven thousand sheep. In Australia, we have a land area the size of the continental United States, a population of twenty million people and two hundred million sheep. Sheep eat grass and do well in large areas of fertile grassland. A lightning strike on dry prairie grass will produce a fire that can travel as fast as the wind that drives it. Such fires will outrun a flock of panicking sheep and wipe them out. It would also take out any shepherds on foot who were with them. It is an awful thing to see. Safety in such a crisis is found in doing exactly the opposite of one's first instinct. The only safe place in a grass fire is on burned ground. So with the fire approaching, it is best to light another fire and let it run away, and as it does, move in behind it and stand on the burned ground. This simple technique has stimulated many a preacher to see a parallel with the work of Christ, who died in our place. When I take the step of faith and accept Jesus as Lord, I move onto burned ground. Grass can't be burned twice, nor can a person's sin be punished twice. God cannot and will not bring down his fiery judgment on Jesus and then on me for my sin. In Christ, we stand on burned ground. Sadly, these shepherds and their sheep did not.

The third disaster is brought about by a "Chaldean" raid, which took Job's three thousand camels and the servants employed to look after them. Who these "Chaldeans" (*kasdim*) are remains a mystery. They are not the people we know from a thousand years later who were located in southern Mesopotamia. We have no records of Chaldeans earlier than the first millennium BC. It may be a reference to the descendents of Kesed, one of Abraham's nephews (Gen. 22:22; Jer. 35:11) from Aram. Such a raid would probably have come from the north, following the sources of fresh water.

Each of the four disasters may have happened some days or even weeks prior to the day when the news reached Job. The eldest son's house would probably not have been more than a day or two from Job's home. It is an essential aspect of Satan's strategy here that the news of all four disasters be delivered one after the other with no opportunity for Job to gather his thoughts or work through anything. It is necessary that there be a survivor from each disaster to bring the news, and that they arrive within minutes of each other.

The last messenger brings the worst news. This time the assault comes from the desert as what appears to be a tornado. Job's whole family, all his sons and daughters, were celebrating at the home of his firstborn when the whirlwind struck. The picture of the first-born's house being hit from all four sides immediately creates an image of Job, standing in his house, having now received his fourth and most terrible blow. Hartley notes:

> These four plagues revealed to Job that all the forces of heaven and earth had turned hostile toward him. This idea is borne out by the fact that the causes of destruction alternate between earthly and heavenly forces coming from all four points of the compass: the Sabeans from the south, lightning from a storm out of the west,

the Chaldeans from the north and the treacherous sirocco blowing off the desert to the east.[1]

The audience has the sense of a man surrounded and his world demolished.

JOB'S RESPONSE: EXEMPLARY WISDOM (1:20–22)

One could imagine a range of possible reactions. Numb unbelief, total collapse, or more likely a crazed attempt to go to the son's house in hope of finding a survivor—or just to see whether the report was true. But this was the fourth, not the first, piece of devastating news in the space of a few minutes. Assuming Job recognized and thus could verify the identity and reliability of the witnesses who stood before him, by the time the fourth one arrived, there would be little question in his mind but that the reports were true.

So now, what will he say? Will God be the first person he thinks about? Our first instinct is to find someone to blame. Will it be the children? Will he bewail their partying together or wonder whether they had done something terrible to bring about this disaster? Will he want to launch a retaliatory raid against the Sabeans and the Chaldeans? Will he blame the one who designed the house that fell on his family? Will he curse the servants for failing to protect his animals or themselves? Will he blame himself? In this instant of shocked silence, the audience members have a moment to hold their breath as their instincts begin to come into play. Before Job speaks, the emotion in the audience wells up in a number of different directions as the narrator describes the tearing of the robe and the shaving of the head. And it is against these responses that we hear Job open his mouth and repel the shock wave (Job 1:20–21):

Then he fell to the ground in worship and said:

> "Naked I came from my mother's womb,
>   And naked I will depart.
> The LORD gave and the LORD has taken away;
>   may the name of the LORD be praised
>   [Hebrew: 'blessed']."

He said it! He said exactly what Satan predicted he would not say. In Job 1:11, Satan mocks this as an unbelievable option. It was a possibility worthy only of sarcasm—an exercise in hyperbole. But Job said it. Job blessed the Lord. His first thought, his immediate and automatic reaction, was worship.

On July 25, 1993, gunmen burst into St. James Anglican Church in Cape Town, South Africa, and opened fire into the congregation with automatic weapons, lobbing two hand grenades in among the people as well. The carnage was horrendous. One member of the congregation returned to the church, having rushed his dying wife to the hospital, to tell his three children of her death. As he stood in the church building holding these children who had just received the news, a television camera was pointed in their direction, and the journalist asked whether he had anything to say. The broadcast was aired live all over South Africa. Bishop Frank Retief, senior pastor of that church, recounts what happened next:

> Looking into the face of the entire nation of South Africa, he said with tears in his eyes, "I do not know who you are. And I don't know why you have done this. But you need to know that we are Christians, and for Christ's sake I forgive you and I extend the hand of reconciliation to you and I appeal to you to give yourselves up and to become Christians yourself."[2]

As the news teams moved through the church building and the hospitals, interviewing other Christians from that church, they heard the same response over and over. In a country filled with the rage of horrendous long-term suffering and injustice and cries for vengeance, this scene lifted a light in the darkness that brought many to Christ.

The difference between Job and this man in South Africa is that for Job, Jesus was a promise passed down to him through the generations. For us, Jesus' life and work are a part of our history, and we have the witnesses' accounts in writing.

The narrator turns to the audience and announces in amazement (Job 1:22) that "in all this, Job did not sin by charging God with wrongdoing."

ACT 1, SCENE 5 (2:7–10)

Satan's second attempt is horrific. Various suggestions have been made as to the nature of Job's illness. Such attempts are little more than informed speculation. We don't need a diagnosis to get the point. The descriptions in the book of Job are sufficient. Job has boils or painful sores that cover his whole body (Job 2:7). He treats these sores by scraping them with the sharp edges of pieces of broken pottery (2:8). His friends at first either don't recognize him or are so shocked they don't greet him; either meaning would be consistent with the text (2:12).[3] Job reports that his sores are infested with maggots or worms, that he is covered in scabs, that the skin is black and peeling, that the sores are open and oozing pus, and that he has a fever (7:5; 30:30). He cannot sleep because of the pain, and he suffers from nightmares (7:4, 13–14). For anyone who has been in a hospital recovering from painful surgery, Job's description of a night in pain (7:4; 30:17) is

41

remarkably realistic. It recalls pleas to nurses who are not authorized to deliver further painkillers. It is not clear whether the churning he is experiencing in his stomach is emotional or physical or both (30:27). Similarly, we can't be sure whether his statement that his wife says his breath stinks is a metaphor for her having deserted him or a description of his physical condition (19:17). Perhaps given the poetic parallelism with the next line, which tells us that he is "loathsome" to his brothers, it is more likely to be metaphorical. He has lost a significant amount of weight and is "nothing but skin and bones" by the time he is arguing with his friends (19:20). Emotionally, he is a mess. He speaks of being terrified and trembling (21:6). He is crying, his face is red, and there are bags under his eyes (16:16).

In the extent of the physical suffering and in his response, Job points us toward what will happen to Jesus.

For the disciples, the most confusing aspect of Jesus' teaching was his announcement that he was going to be handed over to the elders and chief priests and be scourged and crucified (Mark 8:31; 9:12, 31; 10:33–34). Given their recorded responses to the shock of this announcement, even after it was repeated several times, it is highly unlikely that the disciples even heard the rest of what Jesus was telling them about the resurrection. They seem to have understood something of the concept of the Messiah or Christ (cf. Ps. 2)—the heir of David who would be anointed king and would restore the kingdom of David. Blind people (Matt. 9:27; 20:30–31) and even a Canaanite woman (Matt. 15:22) addressed him as "Son of David," even before his entry into Jerusalem as the king on the donkey (Zech. 9:9; Matt. 21:9). Jesus avoided the title of Christ or Messiah, preferring the more enigmatic reference to the "Son of Man" whom Daniel saw in his vision (Dan. 7:13–14 NASB) of the one who would be enthroned as king and take back the kingdom and give it to the Lord's holy people. Nowhere in this scheme of things could the disciples fit the picture of Jesus as the Messiah, let alone as the Son of Man, suffering and being executed. Neither could any who knew Job's character expect him to end up like this.

It is significant that we find Job, once the illness has struck, immediately removed from his home and from the community and relocated to the town ash heap. To the modern reader, this makes no sense. Why, if you have such a skin disease, would you go to the town ash heap? The question seems even more pointed when we learn something of the nature of this place. This was where the rubbish was burned—and the sewage as well.[4] Under the law of Moses, a person with such a disease would be placed outside the camp or the city as unclean (Lev. 13:46). It was also the place where the ashes from the sacrifices were taken (4:12; 6:11) and where the one guilty of blasphemy was to be taken to be executed (24:14). It is described as a place that is ceremonially clean (4:12). What made the place clean under the Mosaic law was the fact that it was outside the boundary of human habitation, and it was a place where the filth was burned. The remaining ashes then were clean.

It is in keeping with this pattern and set of principles that we find Jesus being led away, in a physical condition akin to Job's, for execution (Matt. 27:31–33). By this time Jesus, too, was a man disfigured. Isaiah's description would fit both Job and Jesus:

> See, my servant will act wisely;
>   he will be raised and lifted up and highly
>   exalted.
> Just as there were many who were appalled
>   at him—

> his appearance was so disfigured beyond that of
> any man
> and his form marred beyond human likeness.
> (Isa. 52:13–14)

God's servant, in such circumstances, "will act wisely." In the passage from Isaiah, there is a double meaning. The word translated "lifted up" can mean both impaled or promoted and placed on a seat of authority above others. For Jesus, the exaltation and glorification began with his arrest and suffering.

JOB'S WIFE (2:9)

Of all the scenes, perhaps this is the saddest. How much more can a man take? Or a woman, for that matter? When tragedy strikes, it is not uncommon to find that one of the things that break under the strain is the marriage. The death of a child, the birth of a child with a disability, or a trauma to a child will often, too often, be made worse when one parent or the other runs away from the situation. For the remaining parent, one tragedy is then intensified, especially if there is the need for ongoing care of the child. Here the children are all dead, and the husband is the one with the disability.

It is possible to read the words of Job's wife as a pathetic call for Job to give up and die with whatever dignity he has left. Again, the phrase "bless God" returns. He has already blessed God (Job 1:21). Will he now bless God under these circumstances? If he does, what will be next? As long as he lives, will disaster follow disaster until he finally either dies or renounces his claim to his integrity? Wouldn't it be better to get it over with? Her language could be a whimpering call to give up, or it could be a vicious and sarcastic mockery

44

of his integrity and his "blessing God." Given the probability that his reference to his wife in Job 19:17 is metaphorical, it seems likely that at this point he loses his closest ally and comforter. She doesn't reappear in the book of Job, and the fact that Job will go on to father another ten children would probably indicate a new wife (42:12–17).

Satan's ambush is complete. Job is not only emotionally shocked and physically disabled but also socially isolated. He is alone on his ash heap.

If we turn again to Jesus, the scene is similar. His brothers did not believe in him but mockingly urged him to go down to Jerusalem and be seen and hailed as Messiah (John 7:1–8). He was betrayed by one of his inner circle. At his arrest, his disciples fled. At his trial, one of his closest disciples denied him with an oath. The words of Psalm 22, only the first line of which passed Jesus' lips on the cross, could also have been sung by Job:

> But I am a worm and not a man,
>> scorned by men and despised by the people.
> All who see me mock me;
>> they hurl insults, shaking their heads:
> "He trusts in the LORD;
>> let the LORD rescue him.
> Let him deliver him,
>> since he delights in him. . . ."
> I am poured out like water,
>> and all my bones are out of joint.
> My heart has turned to wax;
>> it has melted away within me.
> My strength is dried up like a potsherd,
>> and my tongue sticks to the roof of my mouth;
>> you lay me in the dust of death.
>>> (Ps. 22:6–8, 14–15)

Surely this is enough for the man to snap. On Job's next words hangs Satan's case.

JOB'S SECOND RESPONSE

Once more, in case you don't believe, yet: the answer is as deeply rooted as it is spontaneous. "You are talking like a foolish woman. Shall we accept good from God, and not trouble?" (Job 2:10). And the narrator announces again with triumph, "In all this, Job did not sin in what he said."

Satan's case is lost. Or is it?

When ambush doesn't work, the choice is to break off contact and withdraw, or dig in and begin a battle of attrition. Satan is not about to give up.

ACT 1, SCENE 6 (2:11–13)

Satan has now disappeared from the book of Job. His role is taken over by men who assemble with what appear to be the best of motives, but they will turn out to be more like a gathering of vultures.

These men come to console. They must have heard the news, and given the association of their names and their home locations with the land of Edom, it would appear that they may have come quite some distance.

If there is a link between these men and Edom, then that link would possibly bring us back to the hostility between Jacob and Esau, down through the Edomite attacks on Israel and Judah, Obadiah's prophecy, their burning of Jerusalem in 586 BC (Ps. 137), and on to the Herod family as they first attempt to murder the Christ (Matt. 2) and then have a part in the trials of Jesus (Luke 23:11).

The silence of these friends connects with the current silence of Satan. As with the scene at the crucifixion of

Jesus (Matt. 27:45–46), there is a silent pause before Job's voice explodes with pain and a cry to God. They are both righteous. They are both men of wisdom who respond out of the depths of a faith that has unshakeable integrity. But they are also men who feel the pain and the horror of their circumstances.

When people read the book of Job and want to accuse God of sitting in his heaven and playing cruel games with his people, they would do well to look back and forth between Job and Jesus. This is not some Greek or Babylonian god living in the sky and playing games with poor humans. This is the God who became a man and suffered in our place.

The God who baits Satan is preparing his people to understand not only Job's suffering but also his own, when he comes to save his people, and then their own as they are called to follow him and spread the good news of what he will do.

FOR FURTHER REFLECTION

1. Are you apprenticed to Jesus? If so, what skills are you working on as your current focus and challenge?
2. Have you experienced or witnessed any "Job moments"—when several items of bad news struck one after the other? Compare your responses with Job's.
3. How has God been preparing you for a challenge to your faith?
4. Can you discern the hand of God in your present circumstances?
5. If your faith were to be ambushed at this time, where would that attack focus if it were to have its best chance of success?

CHAPTER FIVE

CRYING OUT AT THE SILENCE (2:13–3:26)

S even days of silence (Job 2:13)! Some commentators have suggested that perhaps it was a social requirement for visitors that they not presume to speak until their host should begin the conversation or invite them to do so.[1] Whatever the reason, it would have been a deafening and agonizing silence. Anyone who has spent a night at the bedside of one who is dying will know how dreadful that silence is. There is nothing to do or say for that amount of time that would be appropriate or helpful. And it can be awful. Certainly, for the friends who have arrived, that is their experience.

ROARING AND BELLOWING— THE PASSIONS EXPLODE

The silence, however, is broken with an even more terrible and sudden explosion of noise as Job finally expresses his feelings in words. Job speaks of his "sighing" and his "groans."

> For sighing [*anakhah*] comes to me instead of food;
>> my groans [*sha'agah*] pour out like water. (Job
>>> 3:24)

The New International Version gives us a tame and euphemistic translation of the words Job uses here. "Roaring" and "bellowing" would seem to be closer to the meaning of the text. The first term is used of the growling or roaring of a lion as well as of the Lord when he comes in judgment. The second term is used to describe one who is weeping, or more probably, bawling, at night, in mourning or repentance for sin.[2]

Here it would not be out of place to take a moment to express some concern with the practice of some of our most popular Bible translations, which seem to perpetuate something of a British stiff upper lip, through a well-mannered and well-intentioned censorship of the Bible. Where emotions run high in the original, translators tend to restrain them; where things become too explicit for a Sunday morning Bible reading in a family service, they supply euphemisms. The result can give the impression that our God and our gospel are lacking in passion or reality, when that is not the case. This tendency can be seen in the way some of the language in Job has been smoothed over in the various translations.

Perhaps it is helpful to look at a couple of other passages where these terms are used. So for *anakhah*, "sighing," we find:

> The lions may roar and *growl*,
>> yet the teeth of the great lions are broken.
>>> (Job 4:10)

> My God, my God, why have you forsaken me?
>> Why are you so far from saving me,
>> so far from the words of my *groaning*?
>>> (Ps. 22:1)

When I kept silent,
   my bones wasted away
   through my *groaning* all day long. (Ps. 32:3)

All my longings lie open before you, O Lord;
   my *sighing* is not hidden from you. (Ps. 38:9)

Their *roar* is like that of the lion,
   they roar like young lions;
they growl as they seize their prey
   and carry it off with no one to rescue.
      (Isa. 5:29)

"Now prophesy all these words against them and
      say to them:
"'The LORD will *roar* from on high;
   he will thunder from his holy dwelling
   and *roar mightily* against his land.
He will shout like those who tread the grapes,
   shout against all who live on the earth.'"
      (Jer. 25:30)

And for *sha'agah*, "groans":

How the cattle *moan!*
   The herds mill about
because they have no pasture;
   even the flocks of sheep are suffering.
      (Joel 1:18)

I am worn out from *groaning*;
   all night long I flood my bed with weeping
   and drench my couch with tears. (Ps. 6:6)

Because of my loud *groaning*
   I am reduced to skin and bones. (Ps. 102:5)

This is no whimpering sigh. It is the gut-wrenching howl of a man in pain, knocked down by grief and, in Job's case, overwhelmed by anxiety as well (Job 3:25). Such outbursts are hardly dignified—but then a man in such a state has little thought for his dignity.

One can never really be prepared for the experiences of grief or pain. When my dad died, he died alone in a hospital bed twenty minutes before I was able to be there. The rest of my family arrived within the next half hour. I must have spent two or three days giving people hugs and cuddles and helping to organize the funeral and so on, as you do. As I sat at his bedside alone, waiting for the family, it was as if nothing had happened in a way. He had been suffering with cancer, and we knew he wouldn't last the week. But it was weird because I didn't burst into tears or feel anything. The busyness of the next few days and the grieving of everyone else meant that there was not much time to reflect on things. When I did reflect, I wondered whether there was something wrong with me. I did love the man dearly, and I still miss him enormously. It wasn't till a few days later, when I was alone at home, that suddenly the dam burst. It wasn't weeping, though. It was more like a volcanic eruption. I had to restrain my voice because it would be heard several houses away—and yet there was no controlling what was rising from the soles of my feet and erupting from my face. I recall looking at the dining room table and reminding myself that smashing it wouldn't be a good idea. I wanted to hit something—to fight back at something. But my brain told me there was nothing to fight back against. There was just the pain and the loss, which could not be undone. The outburst didn't last more than fifteen minutes—I don't think my body could have taken it if it had. I howled like the rest of humanity does when, at some point in our lives, the agony of the realities of this fallen world overwhelms us.

I have lots of images of bellowing cattle too, having spent some idyllic holidays at my uncle's dairy farm as a child. One day we came home from town an hour late for milking. There, pushing up against the gate of the dairy yard, were the cows—udders swollen and obviously in some pain. All hands jumped to the work to get the machines into action. But the sight of seventy Jersey cows bellowing is something not easily forgotten. The ribs convulse, then the head snaps into a horizontal position in line with the spinal cord, the nose rises to come into line, and like a rocket fired from a wide tube, the bellow explodes across the paddock and echoes from the hills. What a noise!

And thus we find Job—seven days of silence, and then the volcano erupts. And the audience holds its breath. Will he curse God? In the rage of delayed reaction, will he utter the blasphemy that will make God a liar and prove Satan right? Can a man hang on to his faith and continue to worship God at such a time, in such a weakened and desperate condition?

I can't help but turn my mind's eye to Jesus—not just in his own suffering on the cross either. Probably our most intimate glimpse of the emotional aspect of Jesus can be found in John 11. There it is not Jesus suffering and dying, but his friend, Lazarus. And at first we might wonder whether Jesus is a cold and unfeeling friend because he deliberately waited until Lazarus was dead before he left to answer the sisters' call for help. He wanted to teach them, his disciples, and us, that he would raise the dead. He also wanted to prepare his friends for the shock that was coming their way when he would die and they would have to cope with grief in a new way.

I think if any of us knew that we could speak a word and raise the dead, we would approach the tomb of a dead friend somewhat confidently and without any high emotion except perhaps a sense of triumph and joy. Not so Jesus. As he comes over the hill and sees the people mourning, his emotional volcano erupts. We are told:

> When Jesus saw her weeping, and the Jews who had come along with her also weeping, he was deeply moved in spirit and troubled. (John 11:33)

> Jesus wept. (John 11:35)

> Jesus, once more deeply moved, came to the tomb. (John 11:38)

The words convey a picture of powerful emotions.[3] Jesus isn't just shedding the odd tear. Nor is he upset by the mourners. Nor is he empathizing with them. The word translated "deeply moved" is not commonly used in the New Testament. It describes an emotion more akin to anger or severity than pitiful sorrow (cf. Matt. 9:30; Mark 1:43; 14:5). In classical Greek it is used of the snorting of horses. The second term, "troubled," is also used for the bubbling of boiling water, which is an apt description of an emotional outburst. Many commentators want to rescue Jesus from any display of anger or harshness and suggest that here he is upset by the mourners. But Jesus doesn't address the mourners. Rather, he immediately moves to the tomb and, as it were, goes into battle against death itself. With the power of the Word of God by which all creation came into existence, he orders the long-dead Lazarus to come out—and so he does. It would seem that death itself is the object of Jesus' emotional outburst and that his emotion and his action are in agreement.

As a friend attending a godly family that has been overwhelmed by grief, Jesus is far from silent. Similarly, when it is his time to howl on the cross, the words of Psalm 22 do not proceed from his lips as a simpering sigh but as a gasping scream. The one who stands in the heavens and sets Job up to teach us the gospel was preparing us, as Jesus did his disciples, for the ultimate suffering he would undergo—in our place! It is one thing to wail at a tragedy that strikes a close friend or loved one. It is so much worse when you know it is because of your sin that he was there. So he prepares his people to stand at the foot of that cross and by faith recognize the one who died in our place, and feel the weight of what he has done for us.

UNAVAILABLE OPTIONS

Turning from the passion to the content of Job's howl, we face a similarly confronting set of issues. His monologue moves progressively through three equally impossible alternatives that Job deems more desirable than his life thus far. First, he wishes he had neither been born nor even conceived (Job 3:3–10); second, that he had died *in utero* (3:11–19); or third, that all who suffer might be permitted to die quickly (3:20–26). Throughout this outburst it is significant that he neither curses God, nor does he even raise the possibility of suicide as an option.

While Job's desires are expressed in highly poetic and colorful language, their content is simple. Such desires are all too familiar. And they are equally unattainable. Nevertheless, in expressing these desires Job is being faithful. His faithfulness lies in the fact that he does not step outside the limits God has placed on him and so does not do for himself what God will not do. It is a fine line between wanting to die to escape the pain, and, when God fails to act, taking one's own life. Such faith, while expressing some shocking and horrible desires, chooses the tougher way. There is an analogy between suicide and Abraham's action in taking Hagar to bed to father Ishmael (Gen. 16; Gal. 4:21–31). Behind both actions is the choice to put one's own desires into effect now rather than wait for and accept what God has promised and planned.

It is a hard call. No sane person would choose suffering if it could be avoided. At this point there comes a battle between what is known of the character of God in the gospel on the one hand and our own wishful thinking on the other. Here we need to be careful what we say to people and about people. Some years ago I received a phone call from a friend who had suffered for forty years with cerebral palsy and spasticity of his muscles. He lived in a permanent state of muscle cramp and pain. At age twelve, he had taken his bicycle and gone off for a ride, only to be hit by a bus and permanently disabled. He had come to Christ and was struggling to find his way in the faith. Earlier that day he had attended the funeral of a lady we had known—a lady who had professed faith in Christ—who had killed herself following a messy divorce. At the funeral that he had attended, the pastor had gone on at some length, apparently in an attempt to comfort the family, describing how she had now found peace in the arms of Christ. That night my friend asked me whether he, if he did the same thing, would wake up in glory. The option for him was tempting, if only he could be sure it was true.

In my answer, I told him of another mutual friend who had taken an overdose and, by God's grace, was discovered unconscious and taken to a hospital just in time. She was a believer and continues to profess her faith in Christ. As I sat at her bedside, I put the question to her, "Why?" She said she just wanted to go to be with Jesus. I asked her why she thought that by throwing away the life he had died to give her that she would find herself in a better rather than a worse place? And was she so certain of that opinion that she would gamble her whole eternity on being right? Needless to say, she was angry with me—but twenty years later, she is still alive!

Behind the choice to die must be the belief that the outcome would be better than the present experience, and that death is better than life.

Job here expresses all the things pertaining to what he knew of death that would make it appear to be a better option. These descriptions depict death as either total annihilation, or, at worst, as some kind of unconscious rest (Job 3:13, 17–19). There is no heaven or hell in his description. And therein lies the appeal. In the face of pain and unendurable suffering, to not live would seem far better. So why doesn't he take the next logical step?

Throughout the Bible, suicide is never presented as an option for the believer. Rather, it is the unbeliever who chooses suicide to escape being killed by enemies (cf. 1 Sam. 31).[4] Choosing to live while longing to die is one thing (cf. Jer. 8:3; Rev. 9:6). Taking matters into one's own hands is quite another. Given Job's state of mind, there must have been something more to his understanding of reality that prevented him from taking that step. There doesn't seem to be any indication that he shared Paul's insight (Phil. 1:21–26). Nevertheless, what was true for Paul was also true for Job, whether he understood that or not. And therein is the element of faith as a certainty with respect to things we do not yet see (Heb. 11:1) or even understand. Up to this point the only certainty Job has expressed is his trust in the power and righteousness of God.

Job's faithfulness in persevering with God's plans and purposes was to be rewarded not only in a restoration of his life and attendant blessings, but also with the discovery that there was more to God's plans and promises than he had ever dreamed.

What Satan originally said was God's hedge of protection around Job now appears to Job as a prison wall keeping him inside a life he wishes were over (Job 3:23; cf. 1:10).

LONGING FOR GOD'S REST

At the end of his outburst, Job cries out for "ease" and "peace" (Job 3:26). In the midst of his turmoil he cannot see rest even on his horizon, and yet it is there. When Noah was born, his father prophesied (Gen. 5:29) that "he will comfort us [give us rest] in the labor and painful toil of our hands caused by the ground that the LORD has cursed." Joshua led Israel into a model of this rest, as the nation took possession of a land that was a model of new creation. Into this rest Jesus brought us by way of the cross. And by faith, believing and persevering, we enter that rest. And it was this faith—this persevering faith, even on the slender body of knowledge revealed to Job—that kept Job from giving up on God's way and going his own.

Saving faith is the faith that has as its content the gospel and promises of God in Christ and does not give up (Heb. 4:14–16), just as Jesus did not give up but chose to endure God's plan in his own flesh, to purchase that rest for us.

> Therefore, since we are surrounded by such a great cloud of witnesses, let us throw off everything that hinders and the sin that so easily entangles, and let us run with perseverance the race marked out for us. Let us fix our eyes on Jesus, the author and perfecter of our faith, who for the joy set before him endured the cross, scorning its shame, and sat down at the right hand of the throne of God. (Heb. 12:1–2)

FOR FURTHER REFLECTION

1. Given Job's quality of life and his wish to die, what guidance does Job offer us when we might be in such pain and misery?

2. Spend some time working through the parallels between Abraham's use of Hagar (Gen. 16; Gal. 4:21–31) and suicide.

3. Are we accurately presenting to a lost world the emotional aspects of Jesus, or are we only imagining what was going on in his heart? How do the Gospel writers portray his feelings and passions?

4. Are our emotions in tune with Christ's as we deal with our joys and difficulties?

PART TWO

A TIME TO THINK

CHAPTER SIX

CLINGING TO THE GOSPEL

My students often ask how people who lived before Jesus was born could have been saved. They also ask whether people who have died having never heard the gospel would have been saved. My stock answer to the first question is that people who lived before Jesus was born were saved by believing in the promise of the Savior to come. We who were born afterward are saved by faith in the same Savior, who has now come. In support, I point them to Hebrews 11:24–26.

In response to their second question I point them to Romans 1:18–2:16, and my answer is no. Everyone made in the image of God knows that God exists. We also know that he is infinitely powerful and that we are his enemies. What we don't know, without being taught the gospel, is what can be done to solve this problem. Without a knowledge of the gospel, we would have only two options. We could try to put God out of our minds—either by using a mental anesthetic such as alcohol or other drugs or by creating distractions that will keep our minds off our worries. Or we could create substitutes for God. Naturally, such substitutes would come in the form of gods that are more amenable to our lifestyles and desires. Such gods are, not surprisingly, made in the image of their human creators, and they become personifications of local nations and cultures.

Acts 4:12 is one of many verses that are an embarrassment to those who want to bow before the values of their nation and contemporary culture:

> Salvation is found in no one else, for there is no other name under heaven given to men by which we must be saved.

Job was not such a man.

It comes as a bit of a shock to many people today to be told that we are not saved just by "believing" (as per the theme song of *Prince of Egypt*). Salvation comes by believing the gospel of Christ and not a sincere but vacuous "different gospel" (Gal. 1:6). What we believe is as important as believing it. In every generation, every believer faces the challenge of making sure that we believe the truth and not a pack of lies; that we stand firm on what God has revealed as the way of salvation and don't get dragged down the sewer along with the wishful thinking or traditions of the culture into which we happen to have been born. For New Testament believers, there was the challenge of the Greco-Roman religious and philosophical systems of their day (1 John 4:1–6). In the early stages of the spread of the gospel, there was also the challenge of the "circumcision party" who believed in an interpretation of the Old Testament that rejected Jesus as the Messiah or wanted to live as if he had not fulfilled the promises of the Old Testament (Galatians). By AD 70, there were many more alternative gospels (see Hebrews; 2 Peter; Jude; Rev. 1–3). For Israelites living under the old covenant, there was the challenge of the religious systems and customs of the Canaanites, Philistines, Moabites, Ammonites, Assyrians, Egyptians, and Babylonians; and not surprisingly, syncretism was rife (2 Kings 16; 17:33). Today we face the same challenges, not only from obvious and extreme kinds of anti-Christian opposition that is "in your face," but more particularly from the subtle acceptance of our native culture, nationalistic values, and the customs that teach us to worship ourselves.

Job faced his own pagan culture. Unlike us, he did so alone and without a Bible. So we are challenged to ask how he did it and what his faithfulness might say to us today who have the Bible and are not only surrounded by God's faithful people, but also have the heritage and example of the saints who have gone before us over these past three and a half thousand years.

I think it is interesting that Job is not mentioned in Hebrews 11 among the heroes of faith. That could be because he is not within the red line of the covenant succession, which the author of Hebrews follows. It could also be because the book of Job appears among the wisdom literature of the third section of the Hebrew Old Testament known as the Writings. Nevertheless, it is clear that he was a believer who was saved. God declared him to be righteous before those in heaven (Job 1:8) as well as those on earth (42:7) and commended him as one who led an exemplary lifestyle based on that saving faith. What then could Job have known of the way of salvation? And how much does a person need to know to be saved?[1]

Job's knowledge of the gospel would have been similar to Abraham's, except that we have no record of God delivering any personal revelation to Job by way of vision or angelic visitation of the kind Abraham enjoyed. Surely, if that had happened, Job would have mentioned it in his own defense. It therefore seems unlikely.

Job's knowledge of the gospel would have had to come only through what his family had handed down from one generation to the next. He would probably have heard of the events that we know from Genesis 1–11. He may also have heard of Abraham and of his experiences. He may even have had some knowledge of Isaac and

Jacob, particularly if he had lived after or about the time of Jacob's visit to Laban in Haran.

Clearly Job knew enough of the gospel promises to be saved, so in some form he would have understood what we know through Genesis 3:15. He seems to have specific knowledge of Adam's actions in covering his nakedness (Job 31:33; cf. Gen. 3:10). Thus he would know of his sinfulness and of the fallen nature of humanity and of God's promise to send a savior and to bring us back from being his enemies to being his family again.

Job had inherited a knowledge of the sacrificial system as it was known before Moses, and so he knew about the concept of a substitute who would die in our place to pay for our sin,[2] though his understanding of this may have been very limited.

Job knew one other thing. He knew he was righteous in God's sight. It has been a puzzle to many readers of Job how he could know with such certainty that he was righteous. Many readers see in Job's firm claim to his own righteousness a concept of having earned his salvation by living a blameless life. Certainly his friends understood that to be what he was saying. Today it is still extraordinarily difficult to communicate the concept of salvation by grace to people who have not put their faith in Christ.

This "blameless" lifestyle that Job lived is mentioned several times as a remarkable aspect of his character. Yet, nowhere, even in his most intensely emotional outbursts, does Job claim to have earned God's approval. He defends his righteousness as something that he will not give up, but he does not say that he earned it. Rather, he puts his faith in "the words of the Holy One."

> Then I would still have this consolation—
>   my joy in unrelenting pain—
> that I had not denied the words of the
>   Holy One. (Job 6:10)

He can say to God:

> Though you know that I am not guilty
> and that no one can rescue me from your hand?
> (Job 10:7)

Although he wants to question God and hear from God as to why all these things are happening, Job consistently defers to the righteousness of God and expresses his confidence that God will confirm that Job is righteous. All of Job's hope is focused on God confirming what he believes is a commitment from God already received. But Job has no Bible. What "words of the Holy One" could he be referring to?

Somewhere along the way Job has heard, again most probably through family retelling of the events of Genesis 1–11, how God dealt with people such as Enoch (Gen. 5:24) and Noah (Gen. 6:8) and possibly Abraham (Gen. 15:6). He would have known that people in the past had called on the name of the Lord (Gen. 4:26), believed, received God's favor, been declared righteous by God, and been saved from God's judgment on his enemies. It wasn't much to go on—but it was all he knew of the gospel, and it was enough because it was God's commitment to Job. By faith he took "the words of the Holy One" and clung to them. They were for him all the hope he had in the world with which to face his suffering.

As he reflected on his suffering, Job clung to these five truths.

1. God is sovereign. There is no doubt in Job's mind or in the minds of his friends that his suffering is within the plans and purposes of God (Job 6:4, 8; 7:16–19; 9:5–13, 17–18; 12:7–10, 13–25; 16:6–14; 17:1–6; 19:7–22; 21:13–14; 26:5–14; 27:2–3; 30:20–23).

2. God is just. Similarly, though Job has some harsh things to say about his suffering and the cruel nature of it all, he does not dispute the righteousness or justice of God (see Job 27:7–23), and such a thought was considered a blasphemy by his friends.

3. Job is righteous. Job clings to his conviction that he is righteous and blameless before God (Job 6:2–10, 24–26, 28–30; 9:21, 28–31; 10:7; 12:4; 13:15–16, 22–28; 14:16–17; 16:17, 19, 21; 17:9; 19:4–6; 27:4–6; 29:14; 30:24–26; 31:1–4). He even goes so far as to deliver a long series of self-imprecatory oaths to assert his innocence (31:5–34, 38–40). Job does not deny that he is a sinner (7:21; 14:16–17). Rather, he clings to the concept that he has been declared righteous by God and that he has lived a lifestyle undeserving of such punishment (31:33).

4. God cares. Job's friends seem to have a view of God that would place God so far removed from our experience as to make our sin or our righteousness of virtually no interest to him. Nevertheless, Job clings to the fact that God made us in his image and is thus deeply committed to his workmanship, at least (Job 7:20–21; 10:8–12, 18). Consequently for Job, as for his audience, it makes no sense that God would bring about such calamity on a righteous man (cf. Job 7:12; 9:21–24; 10:1–7).

5. This is really happening. Last of all, Job clings to his sanity and rules out any thought of what we call denial. He is fully in touch with the reality of his suffering (Job 9:27–28).

The problem, then, is how all these five things can be true.

In 2002, the Evangelical Union of the University of Sydney hosted a debate between an atheist, the controversial Sydney journalist Phillip Adams, and evangelical apologist William Lane Craig, on the question of the existence and relevance of God. The following statement[3] by Adams during that debate well illustrates a popular perspective:

> I think God, if he, she or it exists, should be ashamed of him, her, or itself. For the last couple of thousand years it has caused us nothing but trouble. . . .

> I do not respect the Judeo-Christian God because I regard him, or her, or it, as a brute who has created great cruelty and great horror in this world, if he, or she, in fact exists. . . .

> The one thing which we must agree on is that this division which exists between us—in your [Craig's] case over the existence of God or otherwise—should not stop us working together on the important issues involving justice, compassion and decency. At the end of the day, I have to say, God doesn't matter.

In our Western, twenty-first-century culture, the first item to go is the one that ascribes righteousness or any kind of virtue to God. All blame is directed at God, who is deemed unjust and uncaring or unloving. He is, in the thinking of many people today, a monster.

In our Orwellian, *1984* world of "newspeak," we often hear people blame God or even the victims of crime for the suffering brought about by criminals. And one of the worst "sins" we can commit, in this upside-down world where there is no such thing, is to accuse any human of sin.

For others who wish to defend God's integrity, the way out of the bind is to lose the concept of God's sovereignty. They argue that if there was nothing God could do, God could not be held responsible for what happens to humanity. So he could not be considered unjust. He might sit in the heavens and weep with us. He might wring his hands and send messengers to plead with us. But such a god could never violate our divinely created civil liberties ("free will") by interfering with the course of human events. Thus the righteousness of God and the righteousness of humankind would appear to be in place, and the evil power of Satan alone would account for the suffering of the saints. God would seem to have been rescued. But the god who is thus rescued is so weak as to be no god at all.[4]

It was not so in Job's day. Top priority, and the last line to be defended, was the honor, integrity, and reputation of God. There was no dispute as to God's sovereignty or righteousness. The only one of the five truths that could be sacrificed on the altar of rational consistency was the man's righteousness. This one thing had to go in order to rescue God from the charge of injustice. His sovereignty was so far beyond dispute as to not even be an issue.

We might wonder why Job did not doubt his innocence more deeply or why he was not shaken more profoundly in his confidence as to his standing before God. It seems that he reacted differently from the way most of us would have reacted under such circumstances.

The issue boils down to this. For Job to give up on his claim to his integrity would be to give up on his salvation. If that one thing were to be not true, then it wouldn't matter for him what happened with regard to the rest. Job's claim to his righteousness and his integrity were not a claim to self-righteousness but to a righteousness awarded to him by grace and established by the word of promise of God. If that failed, then God ceased to be a teller of the truth and so not a god worthy of the name. Were that claim to be not true, then there was no way of salvation and all was lost. To give up that righteousness and integrity of faith was to lose all.

A person who is not born again will find this concept, of all the concepts associated with the gospel of Christ, the most difficult to understand.

Many years ago, when I was a member of the Australian military, amid the boredom of military life, I happened to fall in at camp with the Roman Catholic chaplain to our unit. Over a number of camps we got to be friends, and I enjoyed many a lively discussion with him. On my bookshelf I still keep the copy of the *Documents of Vatican II* that he inscribed as a gift to me. He was, as people might say, "a lovely man." Certainly he was a man who diligently set about living a godly, gentle, and gracious lifestyle—something many an evangelical and Reformed believer might do well to emulate. So I was upset one day when he took offense at something I said. He was visibly angry and uncharacteristically hostile. Confused, I asked him what I had said or done to so offend him. He replied, "You said you are saved! No one can say that. Even the pope can't claim to be saved!" We talked some more as I tried in vain to get him to understand that my statement that I was saved was not based on a claim that I had earned God's approval by living a sinless lifestyle or paying for my prior sins. He simply could not understand the concept of a salvation that was by grace based on the substitutionary life and sacrifice of Jesus. And so it was for Job's friends and for many other readers of the book of Job today. How can this man be so arrogant, they ask, as to assert his own righteousness and blameless standing before God and cling to what he calls his integrity?

To those of us who have stood at the cross and there understood that God took flesh, lived out a righteous and blameless life in a world gone mad, and then died and accredited his life and his death to the account of his enemies—us—this would have to be the last thing we would ever give up. My righteousness, bought at such a cost, is all the hope I have in the world. And what a hope. And how many witnesses have shared that hope and clung to it with all their being through all manner of suffering and trials, even to the point of death. To deny that is to deny salvation itself.

How important then for Job must have been the family's practice of teaching the next generation about the things God had said and done in their family's history and experience. It is not only the gospel revealed in the Scriptures that we are called to pass on to our children. It is also our family history and experiences that enable the next generation to make sense of a world gone mad. By family I don't mean necessarily our blood relatives, though that is a wonderful thing. No, the gospel goes out into a world of lost sinners who, by faith, are justified and adopted into God's greater family, and as such they share in the heritage of all who have faithfully persevered before.

Each year, when it comes time for my classes to study the book of Hebrews, I assign a project that involves the reading of a Christian biography. At first we hear a few moans and groans. But afterward, every year, we hear of students whose lives are turned around, many who are converted. In a world of self and chaos, without God or truth or purpose, the testimony of the lives of the saints of God who were saved by grace is a powerful heritage.

Without that knowledge, we and our children would have no basis on which to deal with anything in life, let alone suffering. As we are impressed by Job's example we need also to hear Hosea's warning:

> . . . my people are destroyed from lack of
> knowledge.
> "Because you have rejected knowledge,
> I also reject you as my priests;
> because you have ignored the law of your God,
> I also will ignore your children." (Hos. 4:6)

The dedication at the beginning of this work recalls the suffering of my wife's grandparents, and with them of thousands of Mennonites who saw their menfolk slaughtered and their women violated by a man whose name should perish. Handed down to my wife came a diary, written in pencil in an exercise book, by a seventeen-year-old girl—her grandmother's sister. Katrina Hildebrandt died in 1919, among the survivors who escaped the massacre and walked from the Ukraine to Danzig in Prussia. At her mother's knee, Pat heard of the way in which God rescued her grandmother and her sisters and brought them to safety. From her grandfather she learned to read German in cursive gothic script so as to be able to translate the diary in which Katrina described how her father gathered the children for prayer before he and his sixteen-year-old son went out to die. Her diary is full of the words and chords of hymns that express the emotion of a people who knew the gospel and would not let go of Christ no matter what, for to lose him was to lose all.

And so it must be for us, until he comes.

FOR FURTHER REFLECTION

1. How does Romans 1:18–2:16 help us to make sense of the world in which we live?
2. Is the gospel that you believe *the* gospel or "another gospel"? How can you be sure?
3. What other gospels are challenging and confusing the free offer of salvation today? What are the issues?
4. Do you have Job's confidence that you are blameless and righteous in God's eyes? What gives a person that kind of assurance?
5. How would you attempt to answer Phillip Adams's statements? Think about how Paul might have gone about it (see Rom. 1–2).
6. What do you know of the life experiences of those who have been God's instruments in bringing the gospel to you? Plan to find out more about them by

reading Christian biographies, writing or talking to those who knew them well, or getting to know the people in your church.

7. Take the time to write up your story of Christ's work in your life—remembering that it is to *his* glory.

8. How are you helping to equip God's people to persevere in Christ?

CHAPTER SEVEN

THE LAST MAN STANDING

The ambush had failed. Satan's case as presented before God's court was lost. Any hope of victory now would have to be settled outside the courtroom. Perhaps if Job could be isolated and worn down, he might crack and denounce God, and Satan could then return to the court and appeal the result. For this to happen, the accusation would have to be delivered to Job directly. So Satan disappeared, and Job's three friends assumed the task. What started as an ambush had become a war of attrition. The last man standing was surrounded, and the enemy attacked from three sides.

Observing such a war, an audience can be swayed. The extended outburst by Elihu, which begins in Job 32, indicates that the debate between Job and his three friends (Job 4–31) was a public event witnessed by others. We realize that there are two audiences. One is hidden in the background of the narrator's story. The other one is us!

When we read a story like this, it is our natural instinct to imagine ourselves as the hero. We identify immediately with the good guy. But it is a helpful exercise, as we read the long debates that fill the main body of the book of Job, to look for ourselves among Job's friends.

Ever walk away from a conversation that crashed, saying to yourself (or, if you are a man, your wife, who is more likely to know), "What did I say?" We have a string of commercials on television at the moment that show a man doing stupid and thoughtless things because he is so focused on his beer, and when he notices "the stare" from his girlfriend, the response is "What?!"

This is wisdom literature. It is designed to apply the redemption of Christ to sinners and fools. Its best effect is when the sinner repents and believes, and the fool learns. As James says,

> Anyone who listens to the word but does not do what it says is like a man who looks at his face in a mirror and, after looking at himself, goes away and immediately forgets what he looks like. (James 1:23–24)

So before we too quickly cheer Job and jeer the friends, it would be a humbling exercise to listen to the friends and look for our foolishness and insensitivity in their words—and cringe, and confess, and be forgiven. Then and only then is there going to be for us anything like the impact that this book is designed to have, to bless and heal and equip us for a ministry of grace.

It is embarrassing to have been a fool. For Job, the opposite is the case.

It is a great difficulty to be right when everyone else is wrong. Any parent of a child with a high intellectual ability will know something of the difficulties of dealing with such situations—from both sides. When something seems as plain as daylight, and yet can appear as total nonsense to everyone else, there is a loneliness and a consequent emotional confusion that results from being the only one to get it right. There is also the terrible embarrassment of being the greater fool if it turns out that one has been totally convinced that he is right, only to be proven wrong. In such situations there is an internal debate raging: "How could I be wrong? Why can't they see it? They think I'm arrogant or proud or something. Am I? Or am I just crazy?" The assault on Job drives its cutting edge into this crack in his armor.

The battle takes place in three cycles. Job's outburst has given the friends permission to speak, and so they take turns. Job replies to each in turn, to the three as a pack, and repeatedly he turns away from them and the audience and speaks to or about God:

	ELIPHAZ (Job 4–5)	BILDAD (Job 8)	ZOPHAR (Job 11)
FIRST CYCLE	Job to Eliphaz (Job 6)	Job to Bildad (Job 9:1–24)	Job to all three (Job 12:1–13:17)
	Job to God (Job 7)	Job to God (Job 9:25–10:22)	Job to God (Job 13:18–14:22)
SECOND CYCLE	ELIPHAZ (Job 15)	BILDAD (Job 18)	ZOPHAR (Job 20)
	Job to all 3 (Job 16:1–6)	Job to all 3 (Job 19)	Job to all 3 (Job 21)
	Job to God (Job 16:7–17:16)		
THIRD CYCLE	ELIPHAZ (Job 22)	BILDAD (Job 25)	ZOPHAR (silenced)
	Job about God (Job 23–24)	Job to all 3 (Job 26)	Job's soliloquy (Job 27–31)

Throughout this battle, Job clings passionately to all five truths:

1. God is sovereign.
2. God is just.
3. Job is righteous.
4. God cares.
5. This suffering is really happening.

For all three friends it was impossible to maintain all of these things as true. They could not deny that Job's suffering was real. To deny God's sovereignty or justice would be blasphemous. To accuse God of not caring would be to accuse him of random cruelty and so be equally blasphemous. The only truth that could be sacrificed in order to make sense of what had happened would have to be Job's claim to righteousness. They had no concept of a righteousness that could be a gift of God's grace. Their passion for the righteousness of God drove them even to distort the character of God and push him away from his creation and away from humanity, lest he be tainted. So the battle is joined.

FIRST, ELIPHAZ

Eliphaz appears to be the most senior and respected man present. His comment, at Job 15:9–10, indicates that all of the three friends are possibly a generation older than Job. Being first to speak, Eliphaz probably was the most senior. Job is addressing his elders, not just his peers.

Eliphaz speaks gently and approaches Job with a tone of sympathy (Job 15:11). When he opens his mouth he asks permission to speak (4:2). He recalls Job's good works (vv. 3–4) and expresses his sympathies (vv. 5–6). He offers suggestions and advice (5:2–8) and asks rhetorical questions (4:7; 5:1; 15:2–3, 7–16). His manner is gentler than that of either Job or the other two friends. He seems to be trying to identify with Job as he brings his long years and experience to bear and speaks of the things he has seen (4:8–11; 15:17–19, 27). He even recalls revelations that he has had while meditating (4:12–16). He pleads with Job (22:22). In short, he is a caring, sympathizing, gentle old man dedicated to piety and wanting the best for Job. To be seen to take offense at such a man would be highly offensive to any audience. He seems to be a man who would try

78

his best to avoid confrontation. Eliphaz's error lies in the content of what he believes, not so much in the way he expresses it.

I have some fond memories of Cornelius Van Til. One that has always been a challenge to me, and I think a particular challenge to all seminary students, was a little Latin phrase he used to trot out from time to time. Van Til was not known to be shy in his defense of the faith or in finding fault with the theology of others. It was easy, particularly reading his books without having met the man, to get the impression that he was a harsh person. He was not. This patient octogenarian would take on a serious look, lower the tone of his voice, and remind us that we should be "*Fortiter in res, suaviter in modo!*" It means to be firm in the content of what you believe, but gentle in the manner with which you deliver it to others. A tough call, particularly to young theologians with fire in their bones.

People crave consistency. Those excited by the content of their faith tend to be firm in their belief and overly forceful in their delivery. Those who have more of a passion for people can be gentle in their communications and flexible in the content of what they believe. The two then seem to clash, drawing stereotypes of each other and recasting Jesus and God in their own images. I was challenged that Van Til's model of consistency started at the cross where a sinner, saved by grace, knew the awesomeness of the content of the gospel but also felt, and then could communicate, the grace and graciousness of that gospel.

Eliphaz seems to have the *suaviter* without the *res*. With no cross, and no grace in his understanding of salvation, his *suaviter* can't last. By the end of the third cycle, Eliphaz's blood is up, inventing crimes with which to accuse Job. The mask comes off, and the character of the accuser is revealed.

Eliphaz presents a view of God that saw him as being so transcendent as to have no concern or involvement with anything on earth (Job 5:9; 22:2–3). Yet his God is a gentle god who longs to do good and kind things for his creature (5:10–17).

Eliphaz regards the angels and all beings other than God as sinful simply because they rank lower than God. Righteousness, according to Eliphaz, is a matter of the distance of one's nature from God's nature (Job 4:18; 15:15): the lower the being, the greater the corruption. As such, no human being could ever be truly blameless or righteous before God (4:17, 19–21; 15:14–16). Righteousness and blamelessness are, for Eliphaz, relative terms that could be used only to compare one person with another. If, then, a relatively good man should suffer, it would have to be some kind of chastisement from the Lord, and such a man should be thankful that the Lord would intervene in his life in such a way (5:17–26). But to suffer as Job has suffered—such a catastrophic series of events—Job must have committed some great wickedness because only the most wicked would deserve such treatment. God is just. He would never do such a thing to a relatively good man (15:20–35; 22:4). And so Job's protests of innocence, in Eliphaz's way of understanding the world, are accusations against the justice of God. As such they are offensive to true godliness (15:4–6, 12–13). His case against Job is proven in his eyes by the internal consistency of his argument.

In the face of Job's persistent assertions of his own righteousness, Eliphaz is driven to suggest a list of possible offenses Job has committed that would have brought about such suffering (Job 22:5–11; 13–20). These accusations are lies—desperate lies invented to protect the righteousness of Eliphaz's god.

The only possible remedy Eliphaz can offer is for Job to give up everything, especially his claim to innocence, and, like a monk, seek God. He recommends that Job put away his wealth as well as his wickedness, and promises that God would restore him (Job 22:21–30). Eliphaz presents an offer of salvation that can be earned.

As we read the Gospel accounts of Jesus's interaction with people, we can see a similar dynamic. Jesus at first appears to be the good teacher (Mark 10:17–18), the prophet (John 4:19), a teacher (Matt. 12:38)—and all sorts of people are attracted to him (Mark 3:8). They are confused but definitely interested. Like Eliphaz, they have no concept of grace being a gift of God or of a righteousness that could be transferred from one man to another. The concept of a new man being born without sin was outside their framework of possibilities. That the Holy One of Israel, the creator God, would take human flesh and enter a sinful world probably had not entered the mind of anyone in Israel at that time. The more they heard of Jesus and observed his actions, the more he clashed with their understanding of God's character and the way of salvation, and the more quickly they took offense at him (Matt. 13:57; 15:12). Ultimately, they were driven not only to generate a pack of lies and false accusations (Matt. 12:10; 26:59–61) but also to try, sentence, and execute him as a blasphemer of God (Matt. 26:65–66). And the last man standing was struck down by whips, sticks, and iron, but not by truth (Matt. 27:33–56).

SECOND, BILDAD

Bildad appears to be more of a moralist. He is quick to be angry and frustrated and gives sharp expression to his moral outrage (Job 18:2–4). He accuses Job of not knowing God (18:21). He appeals to history rather than his own experience (8:8–10) and to the created order to teach that God's actions always have a cause (8:11–19). Bildad seems to be more impersonal than Eliphaz.

Like Eliphaz, Bildad defends the justice of God, who could not bring disaster on an innocent man (Job 8:3; 18:6-21). He sees God as far away (25:2-3). He also believes that righteousness is a matter of one's rank in the created order, so no other creature, not even the angels, can be pure in God's sight (25:4-5). He sees man as lower than the angels and particularly disgusting because of his low position (25:6).

Perhaps Bildad sees no point in being gentle, since Eliphaz doesn't seem to be getting anywhere, so he goes directly to the issue of the particular sin that he presumes brought on these disasters. In one of the most callous outbursts of the whole debate, Bildad asks whether all this came about because of sins committed by Job's children (Job 8:4). He is outraged at the suggestion that God would so abuse a man of integrity (8:20-21). In pointed irony, our storyteller reads the words of Bildad as he warns Job that God will make fools of the enemies of a man of integrity (8:22).

Bildad's solution is for Job to seek God and live an upright life, and he promises that God will reward him (Job 8:5-7).

As Clines notes,[1] there is irony here. If Bildad were right and Job were to take his solution, Satan would have won his case. Job, in admitting guilt and accepting that his suffering is a consequence of his guilt, would thus make prosperity his ultimate goal and his religion nothing more than the means to that end.

THEN, ZOPHAR

Standing third in line, Zophar is not tempted to display the patience of Eliphaz or to bother with evidence or experience or history. For him it is all a matter of obvious logic. He expresses direct outrage at Job's arrogance (Job 11:2-6; 20:2-3). As far as he is concerned, Job is an ignorant fool (11:7–12). Only briefly, and only once, does Zophar restate the same possible solution to Job's situation that the other two had presented (11:13–15). Rather, his whole focus is to convict Job of sin, because the only way for blessings to be restored would be for a man to live a life without sin (11:16–19). Most cruelly, Zophar describes the experience of the wicked (20:4–29) in contrast with that of the righteous (11:20), and in so doing he virtually recounts Job's experience. Job then is the paradigm wicked man in Zophar's understanding. Most offensively, Zophar declares that Job's suffering is less than he deserves (11:6).

Zophar expresses himself as a man passionately concerned to obtain wisdom. His passion drives him on to distort the character of God to the point where he is so distant from his creation, and from Job in particular, as not to even bother to remember all of Job's sin (Job 11:6).

Zophar begins as a man already frustrated by Job's failure to see reason, and so he is first to fall silent, in frustration and disgust, at Job's stubbornness and self-righteousness. One could picture him huffing and puffing with arms folded, face distorted with moral outrage, unable and unwilling to speak.

BUT NOT REALLY ALONE

For Job there is betrayal here. Intimate friends have a powerful ability to find the most tender and vulnerable point in a man's wounds, and there direct the focus of attack. As some members of each audience might begin to identify with Job before others, we are all being prepared to understand Jesus. With the New Testament before us, we can recall how his friend became his enemy (Ps. 41:9; John 13:18, 26–27); how those who ought to have loved and welcomed him (Matt. 13:57; John 1:11; 7:1–5) became like a pack of dogs closing in on a wounded animal (Ps. 22:16–21), proclaiming their zeal for God (John 19:7; cf. Acts 21:20–24) but doing the work of the enemy.

When Jesus called his disciples, he made it clear that to follow him was to sign up to be betrayed and rejected by people who would justify their actions as arising from a zeal for God (Matt. 10:16–23, 34–39; John 16:2).

What begins in the first cycle as an attempt to teach and convict Job of his sin and bring him to repentance quickly loses any sense of compassion as Job's grip on his understanding of the gospel is seen as blasphemy and a proof of his wickedness. Failing to win the argument, the friends quickly resort to lies, false accusations, and distorted descriptions of the character of God. Alone, Job must have felt like the last man standing, reeling under the torrent of argument but clinging to what he knew of the gospel, without which all is lost. To be a believer in Christ sometimes is to be very alone—as was the One who saved us and to whom we cling for life itself. But we are never really alone, although all others seem silent, since the one who is our Comforter is the Spirit of Christ.

There is an interesting twist on this reality as we read the beginning of Matthew's gospel. When Jesus was born in Bethlehem, he came to the people of Judah as the long-promised Savior. The rabbis and those who knew the Scriptures had no trouble answering Herod's inquiry as to where the Messiah would be born. "His own" people (John 1:11) ultimately rejected him. But from "the east" came men with three gifts. These strangers "from the east" were wise, and they worshiped the Savior and brought him gifts. For Job, the men "from the east" were friends, but fools, and they brought accusation instead. We need therefore to be wise and worship the One who suffered beyond Job's trials—in our place.

FOR FURTHER REFLECTION

1. If you look for yourself among Job's friends, what similarities make you cringe? What do you need to change yet?
2. What part of Van Til's advice do you most need to work on?
3. What similarities can you see between the arguments of Job's friends and the concerns of the scribes and Pharisees as they argued with Jesus?
4. What do you look for in a friend when you are the last person standing?

CHAPTER EIGHT

APPEALING TO GOD'S COURTROOM

A man comes home at the end of a normal working day, opens the door of his house, and finds no one is home. He starts to think of all the places his wife and kids could be and why they might be late. He checks, and, yes, her car is gone. As he moves through the house, he notices a few things in the living room are rearranged. Slightly worried, he goes to the kitchen to make a cup of coffee and finds nearly everything in the kitchen is gone. With rising panic he starts to look carefully room to room and finds that everything other than his personal items is gone, including furniture. The kids' rooms are bare. Then the doorbell rings. It's the next-door neighbor, who tells him that just after he left for work, a moving van arrived and his wife supervised as the movers filled the van. She had the kids with her—they didn't go to school. She was "really strange" and wouldn't talk to the neighbor. No one can tell him anything about where or why—and the weeks go by. Meanwhile, what is going through his mind is very similar to what Job expresses as he attempts to open the conversation with God.

So the man, like Job, sits alone amid tears and rage and frustration. He wonders what went wrong. What did I do? His imagination conjures up a hundred scenarios. He talks to family and friends. And weeks turn to months.

It has been said that when we are in pain or under stress, we go back to being little children very quickly. The more the pain or stress, the further back we go. We are easily reduced to the level of a two-year-old who doesn't have the language skills to put feelings and frustrations into words. The only options are crying and tantrums. At age three, tantrum turns to questions—"Why?"

When the world gets too tough to handle, where does a preschooler go? One hopes there is a lap somewhere to curl up on and howl. Even better, after a good howl, there is a face at the top of that lap who can understand and speak gently and maybe solve the problem. It's a good place to conclude a clash of wills, and it is a necessary rule of thumb for any parent that no crisis be finished without a talk and a cuddle.

In Job we find a man old enough to be a grandpa howling like a two-year-old and desperately wanting to talk to his dad—in this case, God the Father. Here, there is the pathetic passion of a hurt child—or an abandoned spouse. And the question is, "Why?"

Job asks:

"Why have you made me your target?
    Have I become a burden to you?" (Job 7:20)

"I will say to God: Do not condemn me,
    but tell me what charges you have against me."
    (10:2)

"Why then did you bring me out of the womb?"
    (10:18)

88

"Why do you hide your face
and consider me your enemy?" (13:24)

His agony is made worse by the silence of God:

"I cry out to you, O God, but you do not answer;
I stand up, but you merely look at me."
(Job 30:20)

"Oh, that I had someone to hear me!
I sign now my defense—let the Almighty
answer me." (31:35)

What is it about us that we have to know why? Where does it come from, this idea that of absolute necessity there has to be a reason and a justification for the things that happen to us? Even Jesus, on the cross, cries out, "My God, my God, why have you forsaken me?" (Matt. 27:46; Mark 15:34), as David did before him (Ps. 22:1).

THE HARMONIC IN US

It's not just Christians who look up to heaven and ask why. There is something innate, primeval, so deeply rooted in what it is to be human that drives us to want that question answered. Sometimes it seems like the answer is almost more important than life itself.

As we, the audience, hear Job howl why, there is a harmonic within us that is moved. We don't want to know only why Job is suffering: what about me?

Funerals are interesting things. A man or woman might live his or her whole life denying the existence of God. Yet when a person dies, there is a gaping hole. If there is no God, then death, cruelty, and suffering are all natural phenomena lacking any purpose or significance.

There is neither justice nor injustice. Few are so hard-ened as to be consistent about this. There is something essentially unworkable about such a belief.

To know a human being and to see that person die seems an inexplicable and insufferable waste. I confess that there have been several occasions when God and I have had words about such things. But what does an atheist do? Can a person suffer and accept it as all point-less and natural? If so, mother nature is a monster—and a monster with whom God is often confused. Even the hardest heart will weep and question the sense of these things.

Why is that? Surely, if there were no God and if the Bible were not true, we would all suffer without complaint and lose the ones we love without mourning—it would be as natural as eating a good breakfast or getting wet in the rain. Why do we assume, let alone demand, an explana-tion or a meaning for our lives?

Paul explains it best in Romans 1:18–2:16. Put simply, we are images of God (Gen. 1:27)—a likeness that not even sin and death can completely erase (James 3:9). Every time we look in a mirror, we see something that resembles God. God is just, and we are outraged by injustice—that is our nature as human beings. Dogs are not outraged at injustice.

If then we howl our why—from whom do we expect an answer, if not from God?

What then, when we know the gospel, believe the gospel, and cling to God's words, if God is silent when we scream? Is the suffering not enough that we should endure the silence of God as well? If only God would tell us the reason, maybe we could do something to end it—or so we might think. Or maybe we could find a reason to endure with some idea of where it is heading and what it is achieving. But the silence!

Job fills the silence with his own words, as we do, words that rise and fall on the ocean swells of his emotion. He questions God bitterly:

"What is man that you make so much of him,
    that you give him so much attention,
that you examine him every morning
    and test him every moment?
Will you never look away from me,
    or let me alone even for an instant?"
        (Job 7:17–19)

"Does it please you to oppress me,
    to spurn the work of your hands,
    while you smile on the schemes of the wicked?"
        (10:3)

"Why then did you bring me out of the womb?
    I wish I had died before any eye saw me."
        (10:18)

"Will you torment a windblown leaf?
    Will you chase after dry chaff?" (13:25)

"Man born of woman
    is of few days and full of trouble.
He springs up like a flower and withers away;
    like a fleeting shadow, he does not endure.
Do you fix your eye on such a one?
    Will you bring him before you for judgment?
Who can bring what is pure from the impure?
    No one!
Man's days are determined;
    you have decreed the number of his months
    and have set limits he cannot exceed.
So look away from him and let him alone,
    till he has put in his time like a hired man."
        (14:1–6)

All through this Job is clinging to the words of God; nevertheless, all the evidence seems to indicate that God is angry with Job and bringing down on him punishment for his sins. It is interesting that Job does not deny that he has sinned. While clinging to his righteousness, he is forced to put the question to God that his friends are putting to him.

> "Why do you not pardon my offenses
>   and forgive my sins?" (Job 7:21)

The word here translated "pardon" means to lift up or carry and is the word used to refer to Jesus' actions in bearing or carrying away our sin. In Isaiah's predictions that our Savior would be "lifted up"(Isa. 52:13; John 3:14; 12:32), there is a pun as he is exalted to the throne in heaven and nailed to the cross and then lifted up on that wood to be mocked and to die. Job asks God:

> "Do you have eyes of flesh?
>   Do you see as a mortal sees?
> Are your days like those of a mortal
>   or your years like those of a man,
> that you must search out my faults
>   and probe after my sin—
> though you know that I am not guilty
>   and that no one can rescue me from your
>   hand?" (Job 10:4–7)

> "If I sinned, you would be watching me
>   and would not let my offense go unpunished.
> If I am guilty—woe to me!
>   Even if I am innocent, I cannot lift my head,
> for I am full of shame
>   and drowned in my affliction.
> If I hold my head high, you stalk me like a lion
>   and again display your awesome power
>   against me.

You bring new witnesses against me
　　and increase your anger toward me;
　　your forces come against me wave upon wave."
　　　　(10:14–17)

"How many wrongs and sins have I committed?
　　Show me my offense and my sin.
Why do you hide your face
　　and consider me your enemy?" (13:23–24)

As if there is nothing left, Job appeals to God's self-interest. God has invested a great deal of wisdom and energy in creating Job. So why—it makes no sense—would God attack and so injure his own workmanship? He points God to the time when "you will long for the creature your hands have made" (Job 14:15), for surely God does care and love those made in his image (cf. 7:21; 10:8–12).

I DESIRE TO SPEAK TO THE ALMIGHTY (NOT YOU)

To stand before God is a terrifying thing. Job is shaken enough as he sits on the ash heap, without seeing the visible presence of God or entering his court. Before he could present his case, God would have to shield him mercifully from the terror and remove the physical suffering and the damage that renders Job so unpresentable before the throne of God, so he appeals:

"But I desire to speak to the Almighty
　　and to argue my case with God. . . .
Though he slay me, yet will I hope in him;
　　I will surely defend my ways to his face.
Indeed, this will turn out for my deliverance,

> for no godless man would dare come before
>   him! . . .
> Now that I have prepared my case,
>   I know I will be vindicated.
> Can anyone bring charges against me?
>   If so, I will be silent and die.
> Only grant me these two things, O God,
>   and then I will not hide from you:
> Withdraw your hand far from me,
>   and stop frightening me with your terrors.
> Then summon me and I will answer,
>   or let me speak, and you reply."
>   (Job 13:3, 15–16, 18–22)

But then, Job is worried that if he did speak to God, he would get his words all confused—he would appear as a fool before the wisdom of the heavenly court. Even if he were right in his argument, he would appear to be guilty because he would not be able to express himself properly. His fears are not unlike those of any person facing a modern courtroom.

> "Indeed, I know that this is true.
>   But how can a mortal be righteous before God?
> Though one wished to dispute with him,
>   he could not answer him one time out of a
>   thousand." (Job 9:2–3)

> "How then can I dispute with him?
>   How can I find words to argue with him?
> Though I were innocent, I could not answer him;
>   I could only plead with my Judge for mercy.
> Even if I summoned him and he responded,
>   I do not believe he would give me a hearing."
>   (9:14–16)

"If it is a matter of strength, he is mighty!
　　And if it is a matter of justice, who will
　　　　summon him?
Even if I were innocent, my mouth would
　　　　condemn me;
　　if I were blameless, it would pronounce me
　　　　guilty." (9:19–20)

"But he stands alone, and who can oppose him?
　　He does whatever he pleases.
He carries out his decree against me,
　　and many such plans he still has in store.
That is why I am terrified before him;
　　when I think of all this, I fear him.
God has made my heart faint;
　　the Almighty has terrified me.
Yet I am not silenced by the darkness,
　　by the thick darkness that covers my face."
　　　　(23:13–17)

With no reply from God and these questions sounding more like a soliloquy than a prayer or a defense, Job repeatedly goes back to reason and logic. If God will not speak to him from heaven and Job cannot ascend into heaven to speak with God, then he will need the services of a mediator.

"He is not a man like me that I might answer him,
　　that we might confront each other in court.
If only there were someone to arbitrate between
　　　　us,
　　to lay his hand upon us both,
someone to remove God's rod from me,
　　so that his terror would frighten me no more.
Then I would speak up without fear of him,

but as it now stands with me, I cannot."
(Job 9:32–35)

THERE MUST BE A MEDIATOR?

In Job's intense mental struggle, the concept
emerges slowly that for all five things to be true, this
Mediator must in fact exist. If God is sovereign and all
of this is God's doing; if God is just and he has declared
Job to be righteous; if God cares for this image-of-God
man that he has made out of the earth; if this is all
real and not a dream—then there must be someone
who can stand before God and speak on Job's behalf
and present his case. God's courtroom must be a place
where a righteous man can be defended and justified.
So if God will not bring that courtroom to earth and if
Job cannot ascend to heaven and enter it, there must
be one who can represent him in heaven. The logic is
inescapable and forces the realization that this mediator
and advocate must be there. Thus comes to full flame
this smoldering concept:

"O earth, do not cover my blood;
  may my cry never be laid to rest!
Even now my witness is in heaven;
  my advocate is on high.
My intercessor is my friend
  as my eyes pour out tears to God;
on behalf of a man he pleads with God
  as a man pleads for his friend." (Job 16:18–21)

Having knowledge of the whole Bible and having
received good gospel teaching over the years can build
up in us a too-casual, take-it-for-granted understanding of
who Jesus is and what he has done and continues to do for
his people. In the furnace of suffering, when the heavens

are as brass and God seems silent—when even the Scriptures seem like a barren wasteland bringing no comfort or cheer (and there are such times for the believer)—we have to know that our Mediator stands before the throne of God and speaks for us. We may feel like a child waiting outside the room while others decide our fate, but the one on that throne is our Father and the one who speaks for us is our brother—and this is the place where justice is done and truth prevails.

INDEED, THERE IS

The apostle John was passionate to remind the church that even if the believer should sin, horrendous as that would be (1 John 3:4–10):

> My dear children, I write this to you so that you will not sin. But if anybody does sin, we have one who speaks to the Father in our defense—Jesus Christ, the Righteous One. He is the atoning sacrifice for our sins, and not only for ours but also for the sins of the whole world. (1 John 2:1–2)

When Stephen was dragged from the Sanhedrin and stoned to death, just before he died he saw the heavens opened and caught a glimpse of the place to which he was about to go. "Look," he said, "I see heaven open and the Son of Man standing at the right hand of God" (Acts 7:56). There he saw his advocate, the Son of Man. This sinless man, having paid for our sin, rose to be enthroned at the right hand of the Father in glory (Dan. 7:13–14; Acts 1:9–11)—and he is our Advocate and Mediator, our great High Priest, as the writer to the Hebrews puts it (Heb. 4:14). But as Stephen is stoned to death, his Advocate rises from his throne and stands up. Stephen's last words are to cry out with the excitement and satisfaction of that revelation. For Job it was a logical necessity that remained unseen. For us it is a truth brought to us by a cloud of eyewitnesses. And in that truth we find assurance even in the worst of torment. And to him we cry, with hands uplifted, and we know even through the silence that our case is perfectly presented to the Judge of all the earth who will do right (Gen. 18:25).

FOR FURTHER REFLECTION

1. When you pray and talk to God about how you feel, are you honest and lay it out for him, or are you worried you might say something wrong? Where should we draw the line?
2. In what sense is it right for a Christian to fear God?
3. If God is sovereign and everything is going according to his plan, what is the point of praying at times like this? How might Job have answered that question at different points in his life?

PART THREE

A TIME TO ACT

CHAPTER NINE

LEARNING THROUGH FAITHFULNESS

O ne of the most difficult aspects of being a teacher or a parent is when you know the answer and have to watch while the student or child tries to figure it out. There seems to be an overwhelming pressure inside us to take over and show them how it is done or do it for them—in an attempt to help, of course.

Such is the experience of the audience listening to a reading of Job today. With our whole Bible in our hands, knowing the story from Adam to Acts, it is so frustrating to watch and listen to Job trying to work it all out with only his little drop of gospel truth.

Why then do we, as readers, tend to assume that Job learns nothing through this process? Is it because, at the end, God says Job spoke only what was right (Job 42:7–8)? We find ourselves getting confused over some of the things Job says. One minute he seems to be saying things we can cheer. At another, he says something really strange. Some commentators rush to identify multiple authors and sources. Other readers rush to find ways to harmonize and explain away some of these things. Maybe we need to reflect on our assumptions.

Can a person learn more of the truth without sinning or getting it wrong? Must we read back into the beginning of the man's understanding all of the truth he defends at the end?

Clair Davis shared some remarkable insights with his students in the church history courses that he taught at Westminster Seminary. For young men zealous for the truth, church history poses some awkward problems. What did people believe in the fifth century AD about the atonement? Where would they have stood on issues such as justification by faith or predestination, or what about the inerrancy of Scripture? Davis carefully demonstrated that it was not appropriate to examine or judge a man on where he might have stood with regard to a question that was never put to him. Each controversy in the church's history serves to sift the faith of the generation that had to deal with it. We can only ask where people stand on an issue during or after the time when the argument occurred. And so it is with Job.

This concept also helps us understand a difficult verse tucked away in Hebrews that is a great help to believers of any age. It states of Jesus that "although he was a son, he learned obedience from what he suffered" (Heb. 5:8). Our initial response is to wonder how Jesus, who is God and man and who was without sin, could have "learned obedience." Wasn't he always perfectly obedient? And how did suffering teach him anything he didn't know?

In all our debates on the Trinity and the nature of God and Jesus, sometimes we lose sight of something that was a great comfort and encouragement to the first generation of Christians, and especially to the writer of the epistle to the Hebrews. When God took flesh and entered this world as a man, he chose to work within the same limitations under which he calls us to live. His humanity had integrity, and his temptation and suffering did as well. He did not experience life as a man the way a foreign aid worker might experience a trip to a disaster area. God didn't just drop in for a visit. He became one of us. And that meant that the baby had to learn to sit up, talk, walk, and even be toilet trained. Recently a Muslim girl in one of our high school biblical studies classes was talking about why she didn't believe in Jesus. She could not believe in a God who would become a man and need to use the toilet. But Jesus was fully human.

As a youth Jesus had to learn to be a man. Sinless instincts and an undamaged personality would have transformed that learning process dramatically. But Jesus learned by living in this world as one of us. He didn't sin and then learn not to sin. He just learned.

Jesus' knowledge and his skills developed as ours do. When he tells us that he does not know the date of the judgment day (Matt. 24:36), we should not be shocked. If it had been otherwise, then we could look at his obedience and his fulfillment of the law of God and say, "Yes, but what do you expect? He's God, isn't he?" When we look at the temptation in the wilderness, it would seem a joke—nothing more than a set-up. How could God be tempted to worship Satan? But then, put the man before the devil and offer to give him the world and skip the crucifixion—and you have a different encounter.

Perhaps, then, it is a good idea to look again at why Jesus did no mighty works prior to his reception of the Holy Spirit and why his followers had to remain hidden till they had received the same gift (Matt. 3:11, 16; John 6:27; Acts 1:4–5, 8; 2 Cor. 1:22; Eph. 1:13; 4:30).

There are strong similarities between what we see of Job and what the writer to the Hebrews says of Jesus, when he tells us:

> During the days of Jesus' life on earth, he offered up prayers and petitions with loud cries and tears to the one who could save him from death, and he was heard because of his reverent submission. Although

103

he was a son, he learned obedience from what he suffered and, once made perfect [complete], he became the source of eternal salvation for all who obey him. (Heb. 5:7–9)

In both cases there is a development of understanding through the experience of being faithful while suffering.

Immediately we need to be careful. Many who look for a closer relationship with God have concluded that they could reach their goal by inflicting pain on themselves. They have taken the experiences of those who have suffered and subsequently drawn closer to God, and thought it a recipe that they could mix and apply to themselves. Into this is drawn the elements of pride and the self-righteousness of the Pharisees who would powder their faces to impress the masses with their suffering in excessive fasting (Matt. 6:16–17). There is a lie here. It isn't the suffering that makes the relationship closer—it is faithfulness through a life in which we are not in control and for which we can take no credit.

Job's understanding grew not only through the suffering and his faithful perseverance, but also through the stimulation of the debate with his friends. As we, the audience, follow the debates in Job and later in the Gospels, our understanding then should also be sharpened and honed (Prov. 27:17). Job is being provoked to think, and so is the audience. The trouble is, thinking sometimes is uncomfortable, often is disturbing, and can even seem akin to pain—it's as if one's head were about to explode.

It's not just that so much additional information is pouring in. That doesn't seem to be Job's problem. Rather, he is being forced to re-examine his beliefs.

If we are grounded in the words of God, the pain of that process may be fearful, but the challenge to our faith is not—rather, it is to be embraced. It is to be feared only if we let go of "the words of the Holy One," and then nothing is secure and everything is out of control and terrifying.

IF I DIE

As we read Job, our main attention is focused on the question as to how God could be just and set all this up to happen to a righteous man such as Job. But through the suffering, another question comes to the fore. In the face of the silence of God, Job's suffering forces some serious reflection on the nature of death and what lies beyond it. Job begins to reflect on the question as to what would happen if he were to die on this ash heap. Where would that leave our understanding of God's justice?

In Job's desperation, he wants to die because that seems to be the only way to end the pain. For his friends, it is unthinkable for a righteous man to die in a condition like Job's. If Job is righteous, they argue, there is no way God would allow him to die like that—and ironically, they are right in this instance. As Job screams in pain and calls on God to end his life, assurances that he will live for many more years if he is righteous sound cruel.

But then, if he dies, is he right that his pain would end? He seems convinced:

"For now I would be lying down in peace;
    I would be asleep and at rest . . .
There the wicked cease from turmoil,
    and there the weary are at rest." (Job 3:13, 17)

He also seems convinced that when he dies he will cease to exist:

"The eye that now sees me will see me no longer;
    you will look for me, but I will be no more.

As a cloud vanishes and is gone,
  so he who goes down to the grave does not
    return.
He will never come to his house again;
  his place will know him no more." (Job 7:8–10)

"For I will soon lie down in the dust;
  you will search for me, but I will be no more."
    (7:21)

Any concept of a life after death or a time of return for judgment seems to be ruled out by some of the things Job says early in his debates. At times there is mention of a netherworld of darkness and chaos where the spirits of the dead reside—concepts that can be found in different forms in the literature of pagan peoples from Egypt to Mesopotamia in the two thousand years before Christ:

"Are not my few days almost over?
  Turn away from me so I can have a moment's joy
before I go to the place of no return,
  to the land of gloom and deep shadow,
to the land of deepest night,
  of deep shadow and disorder,
  where even the light is like darkness."
    (Job 10:20–22)

"Man born of woman
  is of few days and full of trouble.
He springs up like a flower and withers away;
  like a fleeting shadow, he does not endure.
Do you fix your eye on such a one?
  Will you bring him before you for judgment?
Who can bring what is pure from the impure?
  No one!
Man's days are determined;

you have decreed the number of his months
and have set limits he cannot exceed.
So look away from him and let him alone,
till he has put in his time like a hired man.
At least there is hope for a tree:
If it is cut down, it will sprout again,
and its new shoots will not fail.
Its roots may grow old in the ground
and its stump die in the soil,
yet at the scent of water it will bud
and put forth shoots like a plant.
But man dies and is laid low;
he breathes his last and is no more.
As water disappears from the sea
or a riverbed becomes parched and dry,
so man lies down and does not rise;
till the heavens are no more, men will not
awake
or be roused from their sleep." (14:1-12)

But then Job starts to think about the possibility of a
return from death and of a vindication before the throne
of God even then.

"If only you would hide me in the grave
and conceal me till your anger has passed!
If only you would set me a time
and then remember me!
If a man dies, will he live again?
All the days of my hard service
I will wait for my renewal to come.
You will call and I will answer you;
you will long for the creature your hands have
made.
Surely then you will count my steps
but not keep track of my sin.

My offenses will be sealed up in a bag;
you will cover over my sin." (Job 14:13–17)

Job is realizing that if he were to die on this ash heap, matters would still need to be resolved or there would be no way to hang on to the righteousness of both Job and God.

Perhaps the disease in Job's body had advanced or he was in significantly increased pain, but there is a deterioration in Job's outlook between Job 3 and Job 16. Initially he wanted to die, but saw that as something that would need God's direct intervention. By Job 16 it sounds as if Job is expecting to die shortly, and his mind is turning to consider the possibilities that that would be involved.

REDEEM ME!

One thing is sure, Job does not want to die and be forgotten. He wants his cry for vindication to be answered, and he wants God to declare him righteous before the whole world. He uses language that may have already been a legal convention. He may have known of the custom that required the nearest male relative (the "avenger of blood" under the later covenant at Sinai; Num. 35; Deut. 19:6, 12) to put things right in the event of a murder. So he cries:

"O earth, do not cover my blood;
may my cry never be laid to rest!" (Job 16:18)

Throughout the rest of the Scriptures there is a similar determination that God cannot allow any crime or injustice to go without resolution. For God to be God, there must be justice, and matters must be put right. Indeed, the blood of all of God's faithful servants, murdered for their faithfulness, is said to cry out for God's justice even now (Luke 11:51; Heb. 12:24). There can be no "getting away with it" in a world under God.

As the nation of Israel was being constituted to be a model of the kingdom of God, laws were established to teach the concept of redemption. Later, if successive nearest male relatives were to fail or not be available, eventually the king, as constituted by the covenant with David in 2 Samuel 7, would be the nearest male relative at the end of that line of succession. The one next after him would be God, since the king was called God's son.

Jesus finally fulfills this law and becomes our ultimate kinsman-redeemer. As such, he has four tasks— redemption of the family inheritance (our place in the promised land—new creation); redemption of our persons from slavery should we fall into debt (Lev. 25:25); redemption of our name lest we die and be forgotten (Deut. 25:5–10; cf. Isa. 62:2; Rev. 2:17; 3:12); and redemption of our blood should any crime of violence be committed against us (Num. 35).

In the hands of sinful men, these needs are answered not by a higher justice but by selfish war and personal vengeance. The redemption of blood is corrupted into personal vendetta.

Job seeks no vendetta against God or anyone else. What he wants is vindication and assurance that God stands by his word. Death now looms large in Job's mind. He seems to have given up hope of God answering his call before he dies. So he begins to struggle to conceive how he could meaningfully be vindicated after he dies.

We can observe a tremor in Job's thinking at this point. As we pass into Job 16–17, new possibilities arise. In Job 16:22 he speaks of death as "the journey of no return." His future seems to lie in the grave (17:1). But then he asks:

"Where then is my hope?
    Who can see any hope for me?
Will it go down to the gates of death?
    Will we descend together into the dust?"
        (Job 17:15–16)

In Job 19, he comes upon a solution, albeit only a logical necessity that he struggles to express. Looking beyond his death, he wishes that this call for vindication were set up as an inscription in something permanent such as a leather scroll, or a roll of lead, or even a stone stele:

"Oh, that my words were recorded,
    that they were written on a scroll,
that they were inscribed with an iron tool on lead,
    or engraved in rock forever!" (Job 19:23–24)

Then, as if out of a clear sky, comes this bolt of lightning, as Job paints a picture of vindication that satisfies every aspect of God's character and justice. Bringing together all the seminal ideas he has expressed about his advocate on high and his blood calling out for justice, he cries:

"I know that my Redeemer lives,
    and that in the end he will stand upon the
        earth.
And after my skin has been destroyed,
    yet in my flesh I will see God;
I myself will see him
    with my own eyes—I, and not another.
    How my heart yearns within me!
If you say, 'How we will hound him,
    since the root of the trouble lies in him,'
you should fear the sword yourselves;
    for wrath will bring punishment by the sword,

and then you will know that there is judgment."
(Job 19:25–29)

The only way Job could be vindicated after his death would be if someone would step in and present his case on his behalf. So this kinsman-redeemer must exist.

Further, the matter must be settled on earth. Job has no questions about God's declarations in heaven. His whole confidence is based on God's words that he is righteous, and these words he knows—and, presumably, all of heaven does too. The trouble is, no one on earth seems to know this except Job, so the vindication Job needs must occur on earth.

For this to work, Job would need to be physically present and physically restored or such vindication would not be true to fact. As such, Job would then see God, because for vindication to happen, God would have to respond to the kinsman-redeemer and appear and deliver that vindication. It wouldn't work if only Job's relatives attended this court scene on earth. If "another" were there to see it and not Job himself, it would be a false vindication, nothing but empty words. If Job dies like this and there is no physical restoration, then there is no meaning to the concept of redemption. It might be compensation to the family, but it would not be redemption of Job.

Job is still troubled and his heart is bursting—but his friends had better know that there must be such a judgment day after death, and so they had better not be found siding against the one God will vindicate.

In this outburst, Job is much like the Ecclesiastes, the "Assembler," in the book of that name. If we assume death is annihilation, then nothing has any meaning or makes any sense. All is just emptiness. But if after death there is judgment and justice shall be done, then God's evaluation gives everything meaning. If this is true, then it would be wise for one to keep that in mind from one's youth and not wait to figure it out until the years are wasted in looking for meaning in the creation itself (Eccl. 12).

Job's conception of this scenario has arisen as a logical necessity. He arrives at it only because the pain and the debates with his friends make it impossible for him to walk away from the question—even for a minute.

Yet even then, it is little more than a concept. There is no shouting and release of great joy in discovering the solution. No pressure has been relieved. The pain continues, and the debate still rages. This concept, like Job's righteousness and integrity, is like a tiny diamond, thought by some to be glass and unable to be verified. Job clings to it like life itself without any sense of triumph or celebration.

I WILL COME FORTH LIKE GOLD

In the remaining debates, Job reviews the fate of the wicked and the righteous, who both die and are buried as if there were no benefit in righteousness (Job 21:7-13). He notes that compensating one's family after one's death does nothing for the one who died (21:21). He reminds all present that God is judge of all (21:22) and so by implication all must face him—and no one can teach or correct him. And so he declares his assurance that even if he dies, "when he has tested me, I will come forth as gold" (23:10). He wishes that judgment was not a time set by God way off in the distance—if only it was a thing to which we could constantly go for vindication (24:1). Nevertheless, God is sovereign even over the dead—they are not hidden from him (26:6). He reminds himself and his audiences that there is no hope for the wicked—neither in death nor beyond it (27:8-10, 13-23). And so he takes his stand as one prepared to die—and falls silent (Job 30:23).

When Jesus spoke to his disciples of his impending death and resurrection, Peter rebuked him and was in turn rebuked (Mark 8:31–33). The rest of the disciples responded as if they hadn't heard a word Jesus had said. They asked for positions in his cabinet after his enthronement in Jerusalem as king—such was their understanding of what was about to happen (Mark 10:35–45).

Even after the resurrection of Lazarus and others, God's plan for our redemption made no sense to anyone, it would seem, except Jesus. But in hindsight, what an awesome thing it is to see God's plan and preparation and the way justice and grace came together in the righteous man, our Kinsman-redeemer, who died like a criminal to save his people and present them before his throne, on the earth, as the holy ones of God and heirs of a new creation (Dan. 7:21–22; Rev. 19–22).

It is one thing to believe the gospel. But it is through persevering faithfulness that we come to understand and appreciate it.

FOR FURTHER REFLECTION

1. What areas of obedience would Jesus have learned from what he suffered?
2. Learning is often a challenge to our pride. How does Hebrews 5:8 help us to have a Christ-like attitude to learning—a teachable spirit?
3. Think about the similarities between Jesus' life and ministry and that of the early church, following their respective reception of the gift of the Holy Spirit. What difference then does the gift of the Holy Spirit make in the life of the church today?
4. Could you explain to a friend from the Bible what happens after we die?
5. What is the difference between the redemption of blood (Num. 35) and personal vendetta?

6. What will need to be put right in your case for redemption to be put into effect at the resurrection? Compare Job's case and your own.

7. Will you "come forth like gold"? How do you know?

CHAPTER TEN

WHO ELSE IS WATCHING?

Suffering in any form raises a person's emotional pressure and reduces social flexibility and tolerance. The more vulnerable a person is, the more volatile he or she can be.

From age three to seventeen I suffered from acute asthma, which was brought on by any form of exercise or physical exertion. Whatever would get a normal kid out of breath had me gasping for air and wondering whether my next breath would make it. The problem wasn't sucking the air in, but getting the air out in time to have room for the next breath. It is a terrifying feeling. I would stand absolutely still, forcing my diaphragm to push that air out against every physical urge to breathe in—maintaining the rhythm "blow—2–3–in—blow—2–3" and so on, until my father would get frightened enough to call the doctor. There were no inhalers in those days, so we had to wait for the doctor to come and give me a straight shot of adrenalin in the leg. Meanwhile, I would stand there in terror that some well-meaning person might try to make me sit down or touch me and break that rhythm.

When other kids would wrestle around as boys do, I would keep my distance. On one occasion they got me into their mass of arms and legs, and the asthma attack began.

Being the smallest boy for my age and the most reluctant to get into physical things, it came as a shock to some to see me lash out and extricate myself from their game with quite such violence—but I would have done anything to anyone at that point. I needed to breathe. Not surprisingly, at times like that, good manners and kind words tend to be low on the priority scale next to the need for clear communications such as "get back, don't touch me!"

With those memories in my collection, I admit to being more than amused when our pastor recounted the birth of his first child. He and the doctor had both been to Israel, so they got into a discussion about their experiences while his wife went through the last stages of labor and things moved into transition. Shyly he informed the church the next Sunday that he missed getting a black eye by less than an inch. Her reaction had the desired effect on both husband and doctor. From such a gracious lady, this outburst was so far out of character that we laughed till our ribs ached.

So, if ever a person might react wrongly, it would be at such a time. Unless, of course, someone was hanging on to faith in the gospel with the same desperation that I experienced when I was pushing that air out. As Job's three friends assemble and present their arguments, Job's responses need to be understood at a level beyond the abstractions of logic and without the constraints of social conventions.

In pain, our minds will race through logical connections with the haste of a drowning person through water. At such times the urgency of the objective makes good manners seem a threat to life itself. Job's friends come into his view not as lifeguards tossing him a line but as enemies throwing down obstacles to keep him from reaching the surface. It is not surprising therefore to find that he avoids engaging them in the debate and rather puts his energy into fending them off so that he can engage with God and obtain the answer he so desperately wants to hear. Naturally they are offended by his terse rejection of their help.

And nothing makes a righteous man appear less justified than a display of bad manners.

As we read this script, we may find our memories calling us back to the Gospels. If we compare Job's responses to his friends with Jesus' responses to his accusers, we discover something of Jesus that is easy to miss.

Have you ever thought to yourself, as you read some of the things that Jesus said to these people, "Ooh, that was a bit harsh!"? Every now and again it seems that Jesus had a short fuse and would come back with a devastating response that we might think was much stronger than the situation seemed to call for. We remind ourselves that he is the sinless Son of God, that he is, in fact, God in the flesh, and so we look to find something that might explain such outbursts. We know he didn't sin. But if our pastor spoke like that to anyone . . . !

Comparing Job and Jesus, the common ground is their righteousness and their suffering. Perhaps we have never appreciated the degree to which Jesus, the man, was suffering, as he walked this earth and experienced its damage and the state of a fallen humanity, knowing as he did that each step brought him closer to the cross. The temptation to worship Satan and skip the crucifixion was real. The constant crossfire of opponents seeking to accuse him of sin on the one hand, and the mass of people who had no understanding of who he was or what he was doing or saying on the other, would have provoked any other man to some extreme responses. There are similarities between Job and Jesus then that we, as God's people, might need to think about as we, too, are called to face our opponents and accusers.

UNDERSTANDING ONE'S ENEMIES

Job's friends are models of foolishness, contrasting with Job's wisdom. But fools aren't necessarily simple. Citing Isaiah 29:14, Paul writes:

For the message of the cross is foolishness to those who are perishing, but to us who are being saved it is the power of God. For it is written:

"I will destroy the wisdom of the wise;
the intelligence of the intelligent I will
frustrate."

Where is the wise man? Where is the scholar? Where is the philosopher of this age? Has not God made foolish the wisdom of the world? For since in the wisdom of God the world through its wisdom did not know him, God was pleased through the foolishness of what was preached to save those who believe. Jews demand miraculous signs and Greeks look for wisdom, but we preach Christ crucified: a stumbling block to Jews and foolishness to Gentiles, but to those whom God has called, both Jews and Greeks, Christ the power of God and the wisdom of God. For the foolishness of God is wiser than man's wisdom, and the weakness of God is stronger than man's strength.

Brothers, think of what you were when you were called. Not many of you were wise by human standards; not many were influential; not many were of noble birth. But God chose the foolish things of the world to shame the wise; God chose the weak things of the world to shame the strong. He chose the lowly things of this world and the despised things—and the things that are not—to nullify the things that are, so that no one may boast before him. It is because of him that you are in Christ Jesus, who has become for us wisdom from God—that is, our righteousness, holiness and redemption. (1 Cor. 1:18–30)

In every generation those who are saved by grace in Christ must face those who would have us save ourselves

118

or who deny the need for salvation. Sometimes these discussions can be highly stimulating and even profitable. Many people have come to know Christ by bringing the wisdom of this world to the table and asking questions and seeking answers from God's people who are skilled and able to understand the questions and find the answers in God's Word. But Job's friends are not seeking answers. Nor were the Jewish religious leaders who sought to find grounds in Jesus' teaching to charge him with a crime worthy of death. Opposing the gospel is the height of foolishness. It is wisdom to fear God and seek the truth. It is a foolish person who seeks to persecute Christ's people. They initiate a very different kind of encounter.

Wisdom is needed to be able to tell the difference between an inquiry and an attack.

REBUKING THE ENEMY

Before we observe and learn from Job's interaction with the fool, we need to stop and recall that we were once such fools. From whatever angle we view ourselves, we sent Jesus to that cross. We don't view the fool from a position of triumph and pride, but on our knees, as those who have taken up their cross and stand in the queue of those sentenced to die. And we think of those who today take their place in such a queue quite literally.

> Do not answer a fool according to his folly,
>   or you will be like him yourself.
> Answer a fool according to his folly,
>   or he will be wise in his own eyes.
>   (Prov. 26:4–5)

These proverbs leave us with somewhat of a dilemma, don't they? What then are we supposed to do?

Sometimes the only way to understand a passage of Scripture is to go and do it. It is often the case that the skills the Bible is teaching only make sense when you are fumbling to make the right choices and say the right things, the right way.

So, as we wonder about how to deal with fools, we take our seats and watch Job do it.

The first thing we notice is that he doesn't spend a lot of time talking to his friends. In fact, he never directly addresses friends individually. When he does speak to the friends, he speaks to the three of them together. "You" in such speeches is always plural.

Job's initial responses are by way of rebuke. His first rebuke is devastatingly vivid. To anyone familiar with the Australian outback or the landscape of a dry and drought-prone area, Job's language is striking.

> "A despairing man should have the devotion of
>   his friends,
>   even though he forsakes the fear of the
>   Almighty.
> But my brothers are as undependable as intermit-
>   tent streams,
>   as the streams that overflow
> when darkened by thawing ice
>   and swollen with melting snow,
> but that cease to flow in the dry season,
>   and in the heat vanish from their channels.
> Caravans turn aside from their routes;
>   they go up into the wasteland and perish.
> The caravans of Tema look for water,
>   the traveling merchants of Sheba look in hope.
> They are distressed, because they had been
>   confident;
>   they arrive there, only to be disappointed.
> Now you too have proved to be of no help;

you see something dreadful and are afraid."
   (Job 6:14–21)

As the interaction wears on, the friends and Job abandon all attempts at good manners or calm diplomacy. Straight rebuke turns to sarcasm, accusation, and warning.

Then Job replied:

> "How you have helped the powerless!
>> How you have saved the arm that is
>>> feeble!
>> What advice you have offered to one without
>>> wisdom!
>> And what great insight you have
>>> displayed!
>> Who has helped you utter these words?
>>> And whose spirit spoke from your mouth?"
>   (Job 26:1–4)

Then Job replied:

> "Doubtless you are the people,
>> and wisdom will die with you!
> But I have a mind as well as you;
>> I am not inferior to you.
>> Who does not know all these things? . . .
> But ask the animals, and they will teach
>> you,
>> or the birds of the air, and they will tell
>>> you;
> or speak to the earth, and it will teach you,
>> or let the fish of the sea inform you.
> Which of all these does not know
>> that the hand of the Lord has done this?"
>   (Job 12:1–3, 7–9)

Job's accusations are devastating and extensive (cf. Job 6:27; 13:2–11; 19:1–6, 20–22; 21:1–6, 28–34).

If we turn then to the Gospels and review Jesus' encounters with his opponents, we find a similar pattern. Among his rebukes we read such vivid descriptions as

"Woe to you, blind guides!" (Matt. 23:16)

"You are like whitewashed tombs." (Matt. 23:27)

"You snakes! You brood of vipers!" (Matt. 23:33)

Many of Jesus' parables function as sarcastic accusations against the scribes, Pharisees, Sadducees, and Herodians, who sought grounds to bring a charge against him. Their social standing, religious authority, and academic reputations are devastatingly brought into comic embarrassment by the parables and even more so by the fact that they are so slow to catch on to what he is saying, even though they do, eventually (Matt. 21:45).

Behind all of these encounters, Job tells his opponents, "I know full well what you are thinking, the schemes by which you would wrong me" (Job 21:27). The wise and faithful one sees through the words to the intention of the heart and discerns that these are attacks, not inquiries. So we read, "Knowing their thoughts, Jesus said, 'Why do you entertain evil thoughts in your hearts?' " (Matt. 9:4; cf. Matt. 12:25; Mark 2:8; Luke 5:22; 11:17).

PREACHING TO THE AUDIENCE

Confronted with such opposition, Job and Jesus tend to avoid engaging the opponent in dialogue. Jesus knew that the time was approaching when the Holy Spirit would be poured out and that when he came, there would be many who would recall these events and be able to make sense of what Jesus had said and done. Not only would his confused disciples come to understand, but even a few Pharisees and priests would be saved. These encounters occurred for the benefit of others who were watching, who were there because they were inquisitive. It is to the audience that the suffering servant addresses his words because it is there that may be found hearts and minds that might be opening to hear and to understand and to be saved.

So, in our suffering, we need to be mindful of our audience. Whether it is before the court of a hostile ruler or in a hospital bed in pain, we are always being observed—and our observers know that it is in our extremities that they will see such an honest and raw reality. This is where they can see the truth about us and our faith and where we demonstrate the integrity and value of the gospel we believe.

Somewhere in the back of our minds we need to keep the thought that the reason God created us and saved us in Christ was to display his glory and to proclaim his gospel. So whatever happens, that ultimately will be the purpose. That also makes the cost worth it.

So, when in extremes, we need to back our thinking up a bit. Our initial cry of "help," and our subsequent "why?" direct us to God—who then points us to our audience. Sometimes we cannot even see that audience—but we can be sure that no suffering is wasted. And therefore we need to reflect on the relationship between cost and benefit. "What could possibly be worth this?" should be a question we might ask ourselves before we have to endure the hard times. If we turn to the cross, we know the answer—but it is beyond our set of values, isn't it?

My father-in-law sold real estate, and he was a godly and a wise man in many ways—which could explain why he never made a lot of money. He also enjoyed searching the secondhand stores for a good bargain. He was quick to tell his clients and the people who owned the secondhand stores that a thing is only worth what someone is willing to pay for it. "What are you worth?" he would ask—and direct people's attention to the cross.

It's shocking, isn't it? How could a piece of human garbage (us), filled with sin and hate and selfishness and given to some disgusting attitudes and practices, be worth the suffering and death of God-become-man? As in the parables of the lost things (Luke 15), why throw an expensive party to celebrate finding a coin? Why risk ninety-nine sheep to go and find one stupid lamb? It is out of all proportion!

The same God who put such a value on us is willing to use our suffering to obtain similar outcomes that we might not value quite so highly. As I lie there, clinging to him, howling, and facing my enemies, I pause to wonder—has he done this to me to accomplish something that he sees as worth this? And I wonder—what could that be? And I look to see who is watching.

I want to turn quickly from my accusers and from the fool and speak to those people. I want it to be worth it. I want them to know Christ and understand this gospel and add their amen to the assertion that this ridiculous and perhaps repulsive human being who is suffering is righteous and holy and loved with such a love by the creator God.

It was with such an understanding that the original disciples were prepared for their mission and the suffering that would come their way.

> The apostles left the Sanhedrin, rejoicing because they had been counted worthy of suffering disgrace for the Name. (Acts 5:41)

> About midnight Paul and Silas were praying and singing hymns to God, and the other prisoners were listening to them. (16:25)

At the worst of times, we want not to waste time arguing with a fool but ensuring that our suffering will be worthwhile and that our audience will know why we are so firm in our grasp of the love of our God—as we point them to Jesus, the One who suffered in their place.

FOR FURTHER REFLECTION

1. Prior to the night of his arrest, in what ways would Jesus have suffered?
2. How can you tell the difference between an inquiry and an attack? How does experience help us to learn to respond wisely?
3. Who makes up the audience watching your life and responses? Would it help to work out a prayer list or a "things to do" list?
4. When our flesh is torn, the world sees what is inside us. Ask yourself, "Will they see Jesus and the grace of the gospel in me at such a time?"

125

CHAPTER ELEVEN

THE POWER OF SILENCE

Children wield enormous power—and sometimes they figure out how it works. When we think of naughty kids we usually think of boys and loud noises and lots of movement and activity. Certainly some lads present us with some challenging behaviors. If we look carefully, however, some of the most challenging behaviors are those associated with silence.

Sarah (not her real name) was a child with a sad story. It was her first day at "big school." At first we wondered whether she had some language difficulties, because she did not speak. Within a couple of days, however, we found Sarah laughing and chatting away with a group of new friends in the playground, and we observed that her language skills seemed to be well developed. In class, all we had was silence.

This behavior is called selective mutism. It is a powerful instrument with which to gain control over one's world. If the child can communicate an element of pathos or is otherwise cute, it is amazing to watch the way all sorts of people and energy are drawn toward them. The classroom becomes a whirlpool with Sarah at the center. As the child's eyes look in any direction, adults and children begin a logical series of questions and suggestions, like so many courtiers wishing to know her majesty's wishes. At one level it is a comic scene; in reality it is anything but funny. For the child there is sadness. For the rest of the people involved there is frustration. For no one is there a meaningful relationship.

After realizing we were not succeeding, we called in a competent professional to put in place an appropriate management plan to change Sarah's behavior. (I hasten to emphasize "a competent professional" because silence is such a powerful instrument that when wrongly used, it can do significant damage.) In place of the whirlpool of attention, the process was reversed. All attention on Sarah was removed. All privileges went as well. So we watched the kindergarten class line up to enter the room. The children were told that they would be practicing good manners today and that before entering the room they must ask, "Please, may I come in?" It was to be a game, and everyone stepped up happily, asked politely, and was admitted— except for Sarah, who stood in her usual silence when she realized her way into the classroom was blocked. She was visibly surprised to be ignored and see the rest of the class, who were behind her, step forward and be allowed to enter the room. But there she stood. She was told that when she was ready to approach the teacher and ask permission, she would be allowed to enter. After a while her desk and chair were brought out to her. She eventually did whisper her request—but not till after a later recess break when no one would notice her whispered compliance. There was a lot more to this process than this simple description—involving safe supervision and a number of support personnel. It is sufficient to note that the only instrument as powerful as Sarah's silence was silence itself.

SILENCING THE ENEMY

Throughout the Bible, God's enemies are portrayed as a noisy horde of raging humanity, too busy venting their evil thoughts and desires to hear the Word of the Lord. Thus Isaiah writes:

> Oh, the raging of many nations—
>   they rage like the raging sea!
> Oh, the uproar of the peoples—
>   they roar like the roaring of great waters!
> Although the peoples roar like the roar of surging
>   waters,
>   when he rebukes them they flee far away,
> driven before the wind like chaff on the hills,
>   like tumbleweed before a gale. (Isa. 17:12–13)

Perhaps reflecting some knowledge of Job, Hannah's song praises the Lord because

> "He raises the poor from the dust
>   and lifts the needy from the ash heap;
> he seats them with princes
>   and has them inherit a throne of honor.
>
> "For the foundations of the earth are the LORD's;
>   upon them he has set the world.
> He will guard the feet of his saints,
>   but the wicked will be silenced in darkness.
>
> "It is not by strength that one prevails;
>   those who oppose the LORD will be shattered.
> He will thunder against them from heaven;
>   the LORD will judge the ends of the earth.
>
> "He will give strength to his king
>   and exalt the horn of his anointed."
>   (1 Sam. 2:8–10)

And David sings:

From the lips of children and infants
    you have ordained praise
because of your enemies,
    to silence the foe and the avenger. (Ps. 8:2)

In the book of Job we can track the path of the gospel and of God's victory over Satan by following the use of silence. Here silence serves several purposes, distinguishing wisdom from foolishness. Perhaps the extended length and number of the speeches serves to dramatically highlight the significance of silence—and in particular of God's ability to silence first his enemies, and then all creation, as the difference between Creator and creature is eventually appreciated. Then argument turns to awe, and worship can begin.

THE FIRST TO BE SILENCED IS SATAN

We do not hear much from the mouth of Satan in the Bible. Apart from the scene before God's throne in Job 1:6–2:7, his only recorded utterances are found in the record of the temptation of Eve in Genesis 3:1–5 and the temptation of Jesus as recounted in Matthew 4:1–11 and Luke 4:1–13. No other words of Satan are recorded in Scripture, although we are made aware that other such conversations may have occurred in Zechariah 3:1–2, Luke 22:31, and John 13:2.

This is not to say that Satan is a relatively silent individual. Rather, his words are spoken in secret. His activities need the cover of darkness. They are discerned as they are worked out in the assaults on God's people. We observe that the words of Job's friends serve to press home on earth the accusations Satan made in heaven. Similarly, in the course of Jesus' ministry, it is made clear that while Satan may be sent packing following his defeat by Jesus at the temptation, his work is continued through the accusations and strategies of those who would eventually bring Jesus to the cross (Matt. 13:36–43; Luke 22:3; John 6:70; 8:44; 13:2, 27). Satan's hand is also identified in the experience of the early church as various strategies were employed to bring down the work of the gospel and stop the advance of the kingdom of God (Acts 13:10; 2 Cor. 2:11, 14; Rev. 2:10, 13; 3:9).

Satan is not ultimately silenced until he and all his are cast into the lake of fire (Rev. 20:10). So when the enemy is silenced in Job, we have a prophetic model and assurance with respect to the promise of that final judgment and vindication of the saints.

THEN THE FRIENDS

The cycle of speeches concludes:

So these three men stopped answering Job, because he was righteous in his own eyes. (Job 32:1)

And Elihu is appalled because

"They are dismayed and have no more to say;
    words have failed them." (32:15)

It is ironic that we first hear of silencing one's opponents from the lips of Zophar, who sarcastically asks Job:

"Are all these words to go unanswered?
    Is this talker to be vindicated?
Will your idle talk reduce men to silence?
    Will no one rebuke you when you mock?"
        (11:2–3)

It is ironic because Zophar is the first of the three friends to be silenced.

131

Silencing one's enemies has two significant dimensions. In the first place, there is the issue of obtaining a hearing. It is the mark of the fool that he speaks and does not listen (Prov. 18:2, 13; Eccl. 10:14). Some years ago I was amused to watch a musician exercise his wit to silence a rowdy member of the audience. As the drunken individual began to call out and interrupt the performance, the musician paused and replied, without blinking, "You'll find your ears work better with your mouth closed!" The humor of the retort evoked gales of laughter. The musician had won the audience's support and embarrassed the drunkard such that there were no further interruptions.

Job, too, found it difficult to get a hearing and had to call for silence (Job 13:13). He also resorted to using the occasional cutting one-liner: "If only you would be altogether silent! For you, that would be wisdom" (Job 13:5; cf. Prov. 17:28). Job was accustomed to a respectful and silent hearing (29:21–22). He received the present noise of his friends as, by contrast, an inappropriate and offensive show of disrespect.

In the second place, there is the matter of the content of the argument—which gospel is true and which accusations will stand. Job's main instrument in silencing his enemies was his skill in maintaining and expressing his faithfulness to the gospel as he knew it. His dogged determination served to so raise the temperature of his opponents' rage and frustration that their eventual silence appears as a combination of exhaustion and cynicism. While they are not convinced, neither are they able to overcome God's man. Their silence is born of futility. Job's perseverance is driven by faith.

Job's skill in silencing his friends may be compared to Jesus' ability to bring the cleverest and most well-prepared arguments of his enemies down on their own heads, silencing them before the crowds and in doing so, publicly embarrassing them (Matt. 22:34; Mark 3:4).

When they heard this, they were amazed. So they left him and went away. . . . Hearing that Jesus had silenced the Sadducees, the Pharisees got together. (Matt. 22:22, 34)

They were unable to trap him in what he had said there in public. And astonished by his answer, they became silent. (Luke 20:26)

The ultimate silence is found in death (Ps. 31:17; 94:17; 115:17), and ultimately it will be in death that all God's enemies are silenced. But Job is a righteous man and so will not be silenced—not even by the impending darkness of the grave:

"Therefore I will not keep silent;
    I will speak out in the anguish of my
        spirit,
    I will complain in the bitterness of my soul."
        (Job 7:11)

"Yet I am not silenced by the darkness,
    by the thick darkness that covers my face."
        (23:17)

THE SILENCE OF DEFIANCE

When eventually the three friends are finished and silent, theirs is a silence of defiance rather than submission. Job has called for the submissive silence of the one hungry to learn. Instead, the friends' silence is presented with the scowl of condemnation and derision. They are unrepentant. Such a place is also a place of suffering and a warning of worse to come (Ps. 32:3).

When Jesus stood before his accusers, his silence was a combination of wisdom in not being drawn into a

133

foolish and ultimately futile defense combined with the defiance of the one before whom his opponents should have bowed. Silence in a subordinate is defiance. Silence as imposed by a superior is disciplinary—and Jesus is Lord of Lords and King of Kings wielding an iron scepter symbolic of his authority to discipline all creation (Ps. 2:9; Rev. 2:27; 12:5; 19:15). His words are like a sharp, two-edged sword cutting deep (Heb. 4:12; Rev. 1:16; 2:12). The silence of God in Job, and the silence of the Son of Man at his trial, is an ominous silence that will sift the foolish from the wise.

GOD'S SILENCE—REVERSING THE POWER PLAY

There is a chiasm or crossover of silences in the book of Job. At the beginning Satan has the initiative (or so it would appear). Throughout the body of the text, God's man and Satan's team argue themselves to exhaustion. The young stereotypical fool, Elihu, vents his mind in uncontrolled noise. Then the Lord appears, and all fall silent.

There is no greater agony for God's people than to find themselves without a word from God. Job's constant cry to heaven reflects the agony of a man who needs to hear God speak on his behalf. His cry is echoed throughout the Bible as God's suffering people look to him for salvation.

> To you I call, O LORD my Rock;
> do not turn a deaf ear to me.
> For if you remain silent,
> I will be like those who have gone down to the pit.
> (Ps. 28:1)

O LORD, you have seen this; be not silent.
    Do not be far from me, O Lord. (Ps. 35:22)

Our God comes and will not be silent;
    a fire devours before him,
    and around him a tempest rages. (Ps. 50:3)

After all this, O LORD, will you hold yourself back?
    Will you keep silent and punish us beyond mea-
        sure? (Isa. 64:12)

Your eyes are too pure to look on evil;
    you cannot tolerate wrong.
Why then do you tolerate the treacherous?
    Why are you silent while the wicked
    swallow up those more righteous than them-
        selves? (Hab. 1:13)

Even Jesus, on the cross, cries out to a silent heaven for vindication using the words of Psalm 22.

Throughout the period of the patriarchs and prophets, as the Old Testament was revealed and written down, God's people constantly went after other gods and needed to be brought to attention by drastic and dreadful acts of God in history. In the time between the Testaments, when there were no prophets in Israel and the visible presence of God had not returned to the temple, then we find a turning and a seeking after God. Much of it was confused and distorted, but a people who once wished to be more like the Gentiles now included a significant number who wished to be identified as separate, holy, and belonging to the Lord. The period of divine silence between Malachi and the birth of John the Baptist effected a change much like our classroom strategy with Sarah. The silence of heaven generated a passionate seeking after God.

FROM SILENCE TO PRAISE

When God visibly appears—the glory of the Lord in the form of the pillar of fire or cloud as described in Ezekiel 1 or Psalm 18—people fall on their faces and withdraw in terror (Num. 20:6; 1 Kings 8:11).

The hope of God's people looks forward to his appearing in glory and judgment:

> But the LORD is in his holy temple;
>   let all the earth be silent before him. (Hab. 2:20)

> Be silent before the Sovereign LORD,
>   for the day of the LORD is near. (Zeph. 1:7)

> When he opened the seventh seal, there was silence
> in heaven for about half an hour. (Rev. 8:1)

Such a scene is not the end of the story. The appearance of the Lord, and his words of judgment and vindication, are rightly received in silent awe. But that awe is the beginning of acceptable worship.

Job is not driven from the presence of God. Rather, he speaks and is heard. The redemption he clung to as his only hope becomes a visible experience of grace and privilege before the throne of God. What follows is worship and restoration.

It is a profitable exercise to review the psalms in which the psalmist confesses his sins or calls out to God for rescue or vindication. The climax of such songs describes the believer redeemed and restored, standing in the assembly of God's people, singing his song, and joining in the harmony of all the saints in worship. The destructive rage of the enemy has turned first to silence before God's throne and then to a symphony of song—diversity assembled in harmony and order, at liberty to be heard in a new way.

And they sang a new song before the throne and before the four living creatures and the elders. No one could learn the song except the 144,000 who had been redeemed from the earth. (Rev. 14:3)

TILL THEN . . .

In the Gospels and Acts we see repeated attempts to silence the proclamation of the gospel—all to no avail. The religious authorities questioned "by what authority" Jesus claimed to have the right to be heard (Matt. 21:23–27; Mark 11:27–33; Luke 20:1–8). Various attempts were made to arrest him (John 7:30; 10:29). Attempts in public to silence Jesus by question and argument backfired. Ultimately the arrest, trials, and execution of Jesus were about silencing the gospel.

Like Job's friends, Jesus' enemies held to another gospel—one in which they could take pride in themselves and their piety. The gospel of grace, to such, is an outrage. If we are saved by grace, they say, then God would be unjust because salvation would not be a reward for piety. What sad irony! The friends accuse Job of being an enemy of piety (Job 4:6–7; 15:4); of accusing God of wrongdoing (Job 8:2–3)—they say his God is too small (Job 11:7–12). Similarly, Jesus outraged piety by breaking rabbinic law repeatedly (Matt. 12:2; Mark 7:5)—and associating with sinners and the unclean (Mark 2:16). He is seen to be a blasphemer (Matt. 9:3; Mark 2:7) because he speaks of God as his father and makes himself out to be in too intimate a relationship with him (John 10:31–39). Those who testify to Jesus' power to heal are ordered to be silent (John 9:34) because they are considered too sinful to deserve such a miracle. Eventually, when the religious leaders realize Jesus is claiming to be God, their rage explodes (John 8:58–59; Matt. 26:63–68). They hope that death will silence this gospel once and for all—and so they yell outside the home of Pontius Pilate—and they crucify Jesus.

With the resurrection, a new crescendo begins. The crowds in the temple gather, wondering what all the noise is about (Acts 2:6), and the number of voices multiplies (Acts 2:41). This gospel is not muffled by prison walls (Acts 5:17–25; 16:25–26) or restrained by jailers (Acts 16:22–40), intimidated by threats (Acts 4:19–20; 5:29), or silenced by murder (Acts 8:1; 9:31). The sound of the gospel expands like a plague, even entering the courts of the enemy (Acts 13:7–12; 17:22–34; 22–28).

And so continues the battle for silence today. It has been my privilege to spend a few weeks teaching the Bible to the saints in Myanmar (previously called Burma). The military government there is hostile to Christians and to the spread of the gospel, so we come across laws that forbid Christians to build permanent buildings on any land that they might own. All church buildings less than a hundred years old were closed, so the Christians moved their meetings back into homes. Then the neighbors complained, and it was made illegal to sing in homes. Christians cannot stay overnight with other believers. But there are more than a hundred Bible colleges in the capital city, Yangon—and the students sing well. We met a pastor there who had been jailed for smuggling Bibles across the border into China. (We had been bringing Bibles and theological books into Myanmar.) Non-Christian neighbors of this pastor told us that when they put him in jail, he had a hard time understanding why God would let this happen, and he was quite depressed and struggling with his faith in the face of his enemies. These neighbors laughed as they recounted how, after a few months, this man was put out of the jail and told to go home. He wasn't so much released as expelled from the jail. In those few months, he had led not only most of the other prisoners to Christ but a significant number of the prison guards as well.

The gospel is the power of God for salvation, and it will break down the gates of hell (Matt. 16:18; cf. Gen. 24:60). This gospel will silence all enemies and bring forth awe and worship in the place of this world's rage. But first we must learn the wisdom of Job to be like Christ, so that we can build on the foundation of the apostles. These stones (Luke 19:40; 1 Peter 2:5) will cry out till he returns.

FOR FURTHER REFLECTION

1. Read Psalm 22. When and why would it be appropriate for this to be your song to the Lord?
2. What efforts do you see around you aimed at silencing the gospel? How should we respond to those in terms of faithfulness and wisdom?
3. Search Proverbs for wisdom on how we speak to people. Memorize only the proverbs that make you cringe.

PART FOUR

A TIME TO LISTEN

CHAPTER TWELVE

BUT FIRST THE FOOL: ELIHU (32–37)

To anyone who grew up in the 1960s, reading Elihu can be painfully embarrassing. For me, Elihu brings back many vivid memories, including my first impressions of undergraduate life at the University of Sydney in 1969. I recall sitting on the front steps of the university library, watching an anti-Vietnam War demonstration assembling on the front lawn. Five thousand people, with placards and banners and a few Vietcong flags, were enjoying the music and listening to the speakers. There were badges and T-shirts, and there was fire in the bones. And it was loud!

It was the custom during the first week of the academic year for the university regiment to put on a display to escort the state governor, Sir Roden Cutler, as he visited the campus. For the occasion, the governor paraded in full uniform as honorary colonel of the regiment. He was a graduate of Sydney University and had begun his military service in that regiment. He went on to lose a leg and win a Victoria Cross in Syria fighting the Vichy French in June 1941. Whatever one might have thought of the Vietnam War, or the demonstrators, or even the wisdom of putting on a military display in the face of the passions of that demonstration, Roden

143

Cutler was a man who was rightly held in the greatest respect by nearly everybody. So when the demonstrators pelted him with tomatoes, they lost all respect and sympathy as the photos appeared on the evening news and in the newspapers. Even those who agreed with their cause deemed them "young hoodlums," "fools!"

Whatever else may be said of those days, university life was far from boring. Everywhere you turned, there were young people passionate about something and not embarrassed or inhibited in any way from sharing their opinions. Getting into a theological argument was about as hard as breathing. Avoiding theological argument was almost impossible. For those facing compulsory military call-up, what you believed and the choices you made, back then, could cost you your life. Such consequences tend to focus the heart and mind.

There is something essential to being young that brings out the enthusiasm and passion of any issue. Older and supposedly wiser heads can, and often do, appear to be conniving, cowardly, patronizing, arrogant, hypocritical, dishonest—the list goes on, doesn't it? We think we are the first generation to ever feel like this or spot these deficiencies in our elders. Discovering that this has been the way of humanity for all generations somehow only fuels the fire.

In one of my seventeen-year-old Elihu moments, my pastor took me aside and said, "David—don't tell us what we're doing wrong. Show us what will work better." What was wrong was wrong—and it was so frustrating. But the truth was, none of us could think of anything that would work better, including me. I was just venting what everyone felt—and that didn't help anyone.

For the reader or the audience who have been listening through to the end of Job's final soliloquy, the issues are exhausted without resolution. The speeches have become more aggressive and louder, and the atmosphere is about as tense as it could get. Elihu's speech drops on us with the full force of comic relief—the kind that works best when the pressure is at its height. His comments fall on the ear like gunshots in a still night. You say to yourself—"Did he really say what I just heard?" He is the ultimate young fool, and his speech restores Job's dignity by default. He also sinks the case for the three friends. By the time he is through his first outburst, the audience is either aching with laughter or storming the stage. By the end of his fourth, they are silent in anticipation of God's looming judgment, aware that Elihu doesn't see it coming.

THE ANGRY YOUNG MAN RISES

We should extend some sympathy to Elihu as he rises to his feet. As an audience, we are exhausted and dissatisfied. The questions are still swirling around in our heads, and we don't see an answer yet. It has been a long and emotional exchange. Job is a pathetic figure. His friends are silent and sullen. And this young man has been sitting there all this time respectfully listening and hoping that these elders would close the deal with Job. There they are, like three big preschoolers, enraged and all too aware that they are powerless. The disappointment is to the point of embarrassment. What misplaced hope and respect Elihu had invested in these men!

In Job 32:1-5 the narrator returns, in a short prose interlude, to introduce Elihu to the audience. Four times, in those few verses, he tells us that Elihu is angry—at Job and at the three friends. He is angry at Job for his persistent claim to be righteous before God. He is angry at the three friends for failing to win the argument. In Elihu's eyes, the matter is so simple and obvious it is beyond absurdity that these men couldn't make Job see it as it is.

A BELLY FULL OF GAS

The tongue of the wise commends knowledge,
    but the mouth of the fool gushes folly.
        (Prov. 15:2)

One lesson preachers need to learn early is that if you have something to say, get on with it. Elihu spends almost a quarter of his time telling us why we should listen to him—and all he has managed to say is that he can do what everyone else failed to do. Oh, yes—and that he is bursting with things to say. And so we come to his first blooper:

"I too will have my say;
    I too will tell what I know.
For I am full of words,
    and the spirit within me compels me;
inside I am like bottled-up wine,
    like new wineskins ready to burst.
I must speak and find relief;
    I must open my lips and reply." (Job 32:17–20)

The New International Version translates the second line of verse 18 euphemistically. Literally Elihu is saying that "the wind [Hebrew *ruakh*] in my belly is under pressure."

For those in the audience with good memories, there is irony in much of what Elihu says—none more pointed than here. Recall these lines, keeping in mind that the word for belly and for womb is the same:

Bildad to Job, Round One:

"How long will you say such things?
    Your words are a blustering wind." (Job 8:2)

Zophar to Job, Round One:

146

"Are all these [literally, "a multitude of"] words to
    go unanswered?
  Is this talker to be vindicated?" (11:2)

Eliphaz to Job, Round Two:

"Would a wise man answer with empty notions
    or fill his belly with the hot east wind?" (15:2)

They [the godless] conceive trouble and give birth
    to evil;
  their womb [belly] fashions deceit. (15:35)

Job to Eliphaz and the others, Round Two:

"I have heard many things like these;
    miserable comforters are you all!
  Will your long-winded speeches never end?
    What ails you that you keep on arguing?"
    (16:2–3)

Being a windbag, up to this point, has been an
accusation exchanged by both sides, but for Elihu it
is something in which to boast. Not only that, but in
Elihu's form of expression, the image presented requires
a euphemism in translation if this passage is going to be
read in a Sunday service. How embarrassing! To come
out with such a blooper, just after telling off the most
respected elders in the community, in front of an audience—the mood among the onlookers at this point must
have lightened significantly.

ONE PERFECT IN KNOWLEDGE IS HERE

Elihu displays, in extreme form, the mistakes of the
fool. As the proverbs say:

147

> The way of a fool seems right to him,
> but a wise man listens to advice. (Prov. 12:15)

> A fool finds no pleasure in understanding
> but delights in airing his own opinions.
> (Prov. 18:2)

If I were casting for an actor to take the role of Elihu I think we would be looking for a seventeen-year-old male, with a body that makes one wonder about his use of steroids, and an attitude to match; a face that would make all the girls melt, probably a top academic record as well, and who evidently knows exactly how all that works to his advantage. The character Joe in *Ten Things I Hate About You* comes to mind, as he expects all the girls to count it a privilege for him to use them and toss them away when done. Like Joe, Elihu is a guy begging to be cut off at the knees. So how much does the audience enjoy watching him do it to himself! Here are another couple of lines where we turn to each other and say, "Is that really what he said?"

> "Be assured that my words are not false;
> one perfect in knowledge is with you."
> (Job 36:4)

And it is not as if he doesn't know better, because later he will say:

> "Do you know how the clouds hang poised,
> those wonders of him [God] who is perfect in
> knowledge?" (Job 37:16)

This, in a speech accusing Job of putting himself up as better than God (Job 32:2), takes the breath away. But we have been prepared for this expression of Elihu's opinion of himself. From the outset we are told, "you ain't seen nothin' yet." Job may have been able to tie these old men in knots, but he hasn't met the likes of Elihu:

> "I gave you my full attention.
> But not one of you has proved Job wrong;
>> none of you has answered his arguments.
> Do not say, 'We have found wisdom;
>> let God refute him, not man.'
> But Job has not marshaled his words against
>> me,
>> and I will not answer him with your argu-
>>> ments." (Job 32:12–14)

In the midst of an exhaustive and exhausting attempt to convict Job of a sin worthy of such suffering, Elihu announces his own righteousness by contrast:

> "My words come from an upright heart;
>> my lips sincerely speak what I know."
>> (Job 33:3)

And, as in all academic disputes, all true scholars and mainstream authorities identify with "me":

> "Men of understanding declare,
>> wise men who hear me say to me . . ."
>> (Job 34:34)

Elihu is the world authority on this subject, isn't he?

By now there can be no doubt but that this kid is going to go down in a big way.

TRUE BUT IRRELEVANT

In overwhelming simplicity, Elihu sees the question as a no-brainer. Job has advanced five assertions:

1. God is sovereign.
2. God is just.
3. Job is righteous.
4. God cares.
5. This is really happening.

All five points cannot be true. There can be no question as to which item on the list has to go. So what's the problem? For Elihu there can be no problem. All that is needed is to put enough pressure on number three, and the matter should be resolved. Any other alternative is either blasphemous or insane.

Like the three friends before him, as Elihu tries to suppress Job's claim to righteousness, he distorts the sovereignty of God. It's like squeezing a balloon. Elihu is sure that there is more than one balloon and that he can burst the one with Job's righteousness on it. Job is sure that all five truths are just aspects of the one gospel—and he is right. So Elihu rolls up his sleeves and goes to work—for four speeches and six chapters! Most of what he says is true but irrelevant.

Like many a young zealot, much of what this young man has to say is sound doctrine. He asserts the distinction between the Creator and the creature (Job 33:4); he has a pretty good grasp of "the priesthood of all believers" (33:6) and puts his trust in the truth of his teaching rather than in his rhetorical skills or personal presence (33:7). He is aware that God reveals himself to people in words at various times and in different ways (33:13–15). He asserts God's desire to bring people to repentance and see them saved from hell (33:16–18). He even holds out the possibility of a ransom being presented to redeem a man from the judgment of God (33:23–25). The prayers of the ransomed are accepted, and they proclaim their salvation in the assembly (33:26–28). God is patient and longsuffering and rescues people from going to hell many times (33:29–30). Which is all true but irrelevant.

Elihu distorts Job's words (Job 33:9–11; 35:1–3). His logic forces on him the necessity of believing that Job must have done something terrible, so he is certain that by simply naming such crimes he will be rightly accusing Job. It is a logical necessity and must be so. He claims that Job walks in the way of sinners (34:8–9, 34–37; 36:17) because that's what you do if you have nothing to gain by being faithful to the Lord, isn't it?

In this assertion Elihu is teaching as orthodoxy the same assertion Satan made at the outset—that the purpose of putting one's faith in the Lord is to get the benefits that come with the relationship here and now. Here is a prosperity theology outraged at the possibility of an alternative as if it made God out to be unjust. And yet Job ultimately will prosper—true but irrelevant.

That isn't the question. The question is why Job suffers at all, let alone to such a degree, and why a righteous man would ever be in such a condition!

Elihu evidently enjoys expanding on the fact that God knows all and sees all (Job 34:21–25). He delights in recalling God's justice in taking down the mighty men who oppress the poor (34:24–30)—true but irrelevant.

Elihu's God is so exalted and transcendent that he is not affected either by a man's sin or by his righteousness (Job 35:6–8). Elihu is attempting to present the concept of the aseity of God, in his way. At best all we can say is—true but irrelevant.

God does respond to the cries of the wicked. He is not impressed by false religion (Job 35:9–13)—true but irrelevant.

Elihu waxes eloquent on the justness of God and his power to deal with the wicked (Job 36:5–6). He delights in the possibility of repentance and the promise of prosperity for the faithful (36:7, 11). The concept of covenant blessings conditional on covenant faithfulness is not far from Elihu. At its best interpretation these concepts are true but irrelevant. At worst Elihu is a man who would prove Satan right.

Elihu fears God, and in his youth he has turned to God. He does not want to face the consequences of refusing God's call for repentance (Job 36:12–16)—true but irrelevant.

He says it is wrong for a man to argue with God or to want to hold a conversation in which he would argue his innocence. Such a thought is scandalous to Elihu and proves Job to be an arrogant and wicked man (Job 36:18–23).

Eventually Elihu begins a crescendo of excitement as he describes the sovereignty and glory of the Creator as he might appear in his glory cloud (Job 36:24–37:24), as if to say, "Is this what you want to see, Job?"

At last Elihu falls silent, facing an audience whose expressions have changed dramatically. They are all silent. There is no applause. There is no response from Job or the friends. No one seems to be paying the least attention to Elihu.

HE'S BEHIND YOU

When I was at high school, we had a fearsome deputy principal. His nickname was "Boris"—after Boris Karloff, an old movie star who played fearful roles in horror movies. Our deputy principal had a distinctive voice and turn of expression and was wont to adopt a strange pose with one hand on his hip and his head tilted to the side when he addressed a student. One day our teacher didn't show up for class, and we were getting as restless as any class of fourteen-year-old boys might. One of our number, a gifted humorist and impersonator, took it on himself to replace the teacher as the deputy would do in emergencies. And so we had a full and hilarious performance of "Boris" to keep us entertained while we waited. The only problem was that the real Boris had arrived and had been standing out of sight, just outside the door, for most of the performance. After a while, he quietly slipped through the doorway, finger on lips, warning us not to give him away. I don't recall the outcome—but I will never forget the look on our humorist's face when he realized who was standing behind him.

Elihu has given us an awesome description of the visible appearance of God. (Other such accounts can be found in Ps. 18, Ezek. 1, and Isa. 6.) Now he turns only to see the One he is describing—and the poor young fool is heard of no more. God doesn't even deem him important enough to address directly, nor does he refer to him at the end of the book. Elihu is humbled by his own obvious irrelevance. He is treated like a child, while God speaks to the men.

YOUTH AND THE LORD

Not all Elihus are young men. But there is something spectacularly exciting about being a young adult and being able to understand and know that you can do things as you look forward to the rest of your life. The sense of being able to change the world is not a fantasy or a mere vanity. Thank God there is truth there. Thank God because our world needs changing.

When my generation hit adulthood back in the 1960s and 1970s, we outnumbered "the oldies." We were the kids born at the end of the war. We had homes and prosperity, education and opportunity—and we had the power to change the world. So we did. And our children live in a world built by Elihus. We railed against the rich and mighty, and within ten years we became the wealthiest, most powerful generation, zealous for prosperity without meaning. We were the Ecclesiastes generation who sought meaning in everything—to excess.

During the 1960s there was another young radical named Cat Stevens. He sang songs about being young and wanting to be heard. He put his hope in the "Peace Train," then, like so many idealists, found it all a fantasy. So he turned to find God—and came up with a theology almost identical to Elihu's. He found a god that runs the world on the basis of "justice." There is no grace—that would be unjust. That would be blasphemous. If you have ever tried to explain the grace of God in the gospel of Jesus Christ to a Muslim, you will have stepped into the drama of Job.

We need young people full of zeal—but a zeal for the gospel of grace and so a zeal that is itself grace in action.

When Jesus was approached by a young man zealous for righteousness, his heart went out to him. He saw in this young man the power of a gospel of prosperity. He was a rich young man—and a ruler of his people. Mark tells us that "Jesus looked at him and loved him" (Mark 10:21). So Jesus told him the truth and gave him the choice that would strip off a false hope and replace it with the real one. Satan would have won if Job had believed Elihu's gospel. We cannot serve God and money (Matt. 6:24; Luke 16:13). The gospel is about grace, and only the grace of the cross can ever truly deliver salvation with justice. All five statements must be true, or none of them—so Job stubbornly hung on.

Will you?

FOR FURTHER REFLECTION

1. Take a moment to review a few of your "Elihu moments." Is there a pattern there that still needs some work?
2. What does the book of Job teach us about how elders and youth should relate in the local church?
3. Are you hanging on to the gospel with a realistic sense of desperation and assurance?

CHAPTER THIRTEEN

AT LAST THE ANSWER (38:1–42:6)

I used to teach in Broken Hill—a town on the edge of the great outback of Australia. Just west of that town is a huge claypan known as the Mundi Mundi Plain. Being a claypan, it is perfectly flat—for more than fifty miles. As you stand there, you realize that the horizon is not a straight line. You can see the curvature of the earth. It's like being on the moon, especially at night. As one of the locals there told me, if you head off a few miles onto the flat landscape, then lie on your back and look up into the night sky, you feel like you have been glued to the bottom of the planet. You have a dreadful sense that any minute you could fall off and keep falling into space. The night sky does not look like a flat black sheet with little white dots out there. Its depth is tangible.

I like to take my family and friends, especially kids on camps, to places like that, and lie there and gaze at the sky, and then read Psalm 8. David understood something of this reality when he wrote it. He must have spent many nights camped out on the Judean hills, and some silent times looking up at the night sky. There would have been no city lights or air pollution to spoil the view. To experience that today you have to "go out back." As he was wrestling through his issues with the Lord, David wrote these words:

> When I consider your heavens,
>   the work of your fingers,
> the moon and the stars,
>   which you have set in place,
> what is man that you are mindful of him,
>   the son of man that you care for him?
>   (Ps. 8:3–4)

To know God, we need to get ourselves into proportion. Lying there at night looking at all those stars, David asked how God even remembers that we are here, let alone individually visits one man—me!

It is worth taking the time to meditate on the enormity of the creation. It helps us to get our relationship with the Creator into perspective. When you are dealing with the One who set the stars in place as a jeweler would set diamonds in a tiara, it doesn't make much difference if you are 5 feet tall or 7 feet tall. David is right. How does God even remember we are here? And yet here he comes in the storm cloud to visit Job. At that point it doesn't matter what they see or hear. The fact that God would visit one man is overwhelming in itself.

THE VISIBLE APPEARANCE OF THE LORD

> Then the LORD answered Job out of the storm.
> (Job 38:1)

No one in that place, at that time, had ever seen, or even met anyone who had seen, the visible appearance of God in this form. Not too many people who have read Job would have, either. As such, Job's audiences are about to

156

discover a whole new meaning to their concept of God. We too need to pause and reflect on what is happening here.

In 1952, J. B. Phillips wrote a helpful little book called *Your God Is Too Small.*[1] It had a teddy bear on the cover! It was a helpful book because it made people rethink their idea of God. In lots of ways, we think of God as if he were a big person, like us but without a body, who is as much a part of the creation as we are. And there's the problem.

When the Lord speaks to Job and his friends, the first point he is making is that he is *not* a part of this creation. So pause and reflect for a minute.

That means God does not have a place. He does not have dimensions. He is not bound by the laws of physics. He isn't subject to anyone's concept of justice or wisdom or fair play. Those things are defined by his character, not the other way around. He created time. When we read in Genesis 1:1, "In the beginning God created the heavens and the earth," it means that that was the beginning of space-time. God, who is infinite and not a part of the creation, created time. To ask what was there before the foundation of the earth is nonsense. You can't have "before" if time did not exist. When God created the heavens and the earth he didn't just create "mass"—the "stuff" that fills the cosmos. He also created the place which that mass fills. Take a moment to think about that one. Are you confused? Try getting a physicist to explain the concept of space-time.[2] It is a fascinating concept. God created it, and we are struggling even to begin to understand what it is.

How then could the Creator, who exists outside the limits of this creation, communicate with us? How could we know him? How could such a God relate to Job, or us?

When God created Adam and Eve he made them to be the images of God (Gen. 1:26–28). That is why the third commandment forbids us making images of God ourselves (Ex. 20:4–6). We are the images of God—living images of the Lifegiver. We are vandalized images now—since Adam sinned and death has damaged us. But we are still images of God (James 3:9). As such, we know him (Rom. 1:18–20), even though we might not want to.

Over the centuries covered by the Old and New Testaments, God has spoken to us in words in the languages of people. He has appeared in both human form (e.g., Gen. 18; Josh. 5:13–15; Judg. 13:2–23) as well as the burning bush (Ex. 3) or the pillar of fire (Ex. 19–20; 40:34–38). This awesome revelation is appropriately called "the glory of the LORD" (Ezek. 1). Perhaps, after all these revelations, it is not all that surprising that John tells us:

> He was in the world, and though the world was made through him, the world did not recognize him. He came to that which was his own, but his own did not receive him. . . . The Word became flesh and made his dwelling among us. We have seen his glory, the glory of the One and Only, who came from the Father, full of grace and truth. (John 1:10–11, 14)

This Creator who exists apart from the creation nevertheless took human flesh (not just human form), became one of us, suffered as one of us, and died for us. Since it did not fit our understanding or expectations, we saw it all but understood nothing—until the Holy Spirit was poured out at Pentecost and we saw the pillar of fire again, as he moved in to live with his people.

AND SO TO BUSINESS

In two stages, the Lord answers Job's request that he be given an audience with God to appeal his case:

> "Who is this that darkens my counsel
> with words without knowledge?

Brace yourself like a man;
  I will question you,
  and you shall answer me." (Job 38:2–3)

The LORD said to Job:

"Will the one who contends
  with the Almighty correct him?
Let him who accuses God answer him!"
  (Job 40:1–2)

Several things are happening here. First, Job has received what he asked. He wanted to argue his case before the Lord. Second, he wants God to tell everyone around him that he is not being punished for anything he has done wrong. Job has not asked to be healed or have his wealth restored. Throughout all these speeches, Job has consistently held on to his belief that he is right with God. In a sense, Job isn't concerned about why all this has happened to him. He wants God to confirm that he has not sinned or done anything to bring on such judgment. He wants his faith in God's words, and his integrity, to be publicly vindicated. Given what has happened, that would take an audible word from God. And now he is getting just that.

Job has talked at some length of how he would go about presenting his case before the Lord. He has acknowledged that he lacks the wisdom and the stature to do so. Nevertheless, he has told everyone who will listen that since God is just, there must be a way for him to present his case, and God would have to rule him to be in the right. He has explored his need for a mediator or an advocate to speak with God on his behalf. In spite of the absurdity of the creature attempting to stand before the Creator and request such a vindication (a blasphemous concept in the understanding of all assembled around Job), logically Job has insisted that this must be possible somehow. Now, here God is. And Job has no idea how to proceed.

> Then Job answered the LORD:
>
>> "I am unworthy—how can I reply to
>> you?
>> I put my hand over my mouth.
>> I spoke once, but I have no answer—
>> twice, but I will say no more."
>> (Job 40:3–5)

But neither does he take anything back.

A BARRAGE OF QUESTIONS

The Lord's two speeches come like bursts of a jack-hammer, serving to smash any sense of pride or self-confidence. Yet we need to wonder: is God angry at Job? Has Job in fact sinned, and are we seeing here the final breaking down of Job's stubborn refusal to repent? Such an understanding would seem to be flatly contradicted by God's statement in Job 42:7, repeated for emphasis, that the friends "have not spoken of me what is right, as my servant Job has." Not only has God said that Job was a blameless man to begin with, but now he vindicates Job and publicly declares that what Job has been saying about God has been right—those very things that the friends and many in the audience would have thought scandalous. What then are we to make of God's speeches and of Job's repentance in 42:6?

It is worth noting that at no point does God state that he is angry with Job in these two speeches, as he does when speaking to Eliphaz (Job 42:7). The rhetoric of God's speeches is profoundly intimidating. Job has spoken boldly to God (as if absent but able to hear) and about God.

Perhaps in his passion he "darkened counsel," or, to put it more colloquially, confused the issues. He certainly has attempted to "contend" with God—the word means to bring someone to court to settle a dispute (see Job 9:3, 14–16). Some of his statements do come close to charging God with doing wrong, such as Job 9:21 and Job 10:4–7. His friends understood Job's insistence on his innocence as necessarily accusing God of injustice. If God were here laying these charges on Job, it is difficult to know what to make of his affirmation that Job has "spoken of me what is right."

Similarly, Job's repentance (Job 42:6) doesn't seem to fit into the flow of what is happening. There are several problems.

First, in translating this as "repent," we are reading back into this word more than is there. "Repentance," in modern Christian usage, is a theological term that includes the concepts expressed by three Greek terms from the New Testament vocabulary (see Westminster Shorter Catechism Q. and A. 87)—one speaks of a change of emotion, a sense of grief (*metamelomai*), another of a change of attitude or mind (*metanoeō*), and the third of a change of lifestyle (*epistrephō*). The Hebrew word used in Job 42:6 refers only to an emotion of sorrow, grief, or despair.

Second, if Job were admitting guilt or wrongdoing, this would contradict everything that Job asserted up to this point, as well as God's statements at the beginning of the story and in the next verse, affirming that Job is blameless and righteous. God specifically affirms that Job alone has been consistently saying what is right (Job 42:7–9). A suggested solution to this problem has been that Job is sorry for the way he has spoken, rather than for the content of his speeches. If so, that point is not explicit in the text, and the reader is left to speculate.

Third, the verb that is here translated "repent" does mean other things. It can mean to be sorry for a person (see Ps. 90:13). On some occasions, it describes a person being sorry about an action (see 1 Chron. 21:15; Jer. 8:6; 18:8, 10; Joel 2:13; Amos 7:3, 6; Jonah 3:10; 4:2)—and so "repent" in this sense is an appropriate translation in these contexts.

In all the instances where this verb is used with this preposition, the preposition points us to the cause or the occasion of the person's distress. So, where repentance is in view, the person repents on account of "his wickedness" (Jer. 8:6), or the Lord relents concerning a "disaster" he was going to bring (Ex. 32:12, 14; Jonah 3:10; 4:2). It is difficult to see why Job would repent "concerning his dust and ashes." It is technically possible that the phrase means Job is repenting "on" his dust and ashes, but this would be an unusual expression.

In many contexts, the phrase means to be comforted concerning a tragedy: David was "consoled concerning Amnon's death" (2 Sam. 13:39); Rachel's voice was heard weeping and "refusing to be comforted because her children are no more" (Jer. 31:15); Ezekiel was to be "consoled regarding the disaster" God was about to bring on Jerusalem (Ezek. 14:22; 32:31). It is in this sense that the phrase is used again in Job 42:11:

> All his brothers and sisters and everyone who had known him before came and ate with him in his house. They comforted and consoled him over all the trouble the LORD had brought upon him, and each one gave him a piece of silver and a gold ring.

It is also worth noting that the Septuagint (the translation of the Old Testament into Greek that was made some time in the three centuries before Christ) and the translation of Job into Aramaic found among the Dead Sea Scrolls (11Q10 xxxvii.8–9) both picture Job dissolving into dust and ashes and have no concept of Job repenting.

We would therefore suggest the following understanding of Job 42:6:

Therefore I melt (cf. Job 9:21 "I despise my life")
and I am comforted on account of the dust
and ashes.

The sense would be that the appearance of the Lord and the things he has said have met Job's cry for God to hear him and vindicate him. This is what Job has been asking for all along. We then need to ask how the Lord's barrage of questions would answer Job's issues.

It would be fair to imagine that as the visible presence of God drew nearer, the audience would be wondering whether God would strike Job down.

"Who is this that darkens my counsel with words without knowledge?" (Job 38:2). The friends are sure it is Job. Job is the one being called on to stand before God and give his answer. For the friends and the audience, it looks like God has come to vindicate them and confirm their accusations against Job.

We might be forgiven if we suspect that there is something of a deliberate set-up. God is aggressively questioning Job, and it is clear that everything they have said about the sovereignty and transcendence of God is now being brought to bear on him by God. As they recover from the shock of seeing the glory cloud and hearing God's voice, maybe after the first speech by the Lord, the friends were starting to think they had won the case in a big way.

When they hear sarcasm such as "Surely you know, for you were already born! You have lived so many years!" (Job 38:21), everyone would be thinking that Job is doomed.

The Lord then takes Job, as it were, on a tour of the cosmos, from the beginning of creation to the constellations in the sky, from the weather to the behavior of animals, and asks what his role is in this. If that isn't enough, he focuses in on two of the most fearsome creatures known to Job—Behemoth and Leviathan. They could be real animals, possibly the hippopotamus and the crocodile, or he could be referring to beasts of local mythology. This long and somewhat repetitious monologue serves to allow the initial shock of Yahweh's arrival to pass and the audience to settle down and take in what is being said.

More and more the crescendo of these questions would convince any audience that God was going to declare that Job was a blasphemous and wicked man deserving of everything that happened. The friends might have even begun to cheer inside when God said to Job:

> "Would you discredit my justice?
>   Would you condemn me to justify yourself?"
>   (Job 40:8)

That may be the spin that Job's friends would put on what Job has been saying, but is that what Job has said? Is God agreeing with the friends? Is God's statement in Job 42:7 an affirmation only of the overall thrust of Job's speeches while expressing offense at significant parts of the detail of what he has said? If so, this is a confusing way to affirm Job's righteousness. You can almost hear the friends in the background whispering, "Amen! Yes, Lord! Bring him to his knees!"

The other possibility, which seems more in tune with the rest of the rhetorical style of the previous debates, would be to see God's speeches as an exercise in dramatic pedagogy. When God first spoke to Satan, he employed a deliberate or polite naïveté in his address. He acted as if he had no idea what Satan had been doing (Job 1:7) or what he made of Job's faithfulness (2:2, 3). It was a set-up, laced with a good deal of sarcastic irony. Here again, as the Lord addresses his servant, is there not an eye to the friends and those who have accused him with such vicious and self-righteous moral outrage? Did Job "discredit my justice," or was it the friends who consistently affirmed that God could not bring such calamity on a righteous man? Did Job attempt to condemn the Lord to justify himself—or did the friends' attempts to condemn Job not support the original charge of Satan and, by doing so, imply that God was a liar? Perhaps we need to see in God's speeches a series of charges that, although directed as questions to Job, were accusations against his friends. When we get to Job 40:12–14, the trap would be sprung, as God tells Job to

> "look at every proud man and humble him,
>   crush the wicked where they stand.
> Bury them all in the dust together;
>   shroud their faces in the grave.
> Then I myself will admit to you
>   that your own right hand can save you."

Job never claimed that his own right hand could save him. But his friends urged him to think that he could save himself by admitting his guilt and changing his lifestyle. Theirs was a gospel of reciprocal justice whereby repentance and right living would restore prosperity, without any concept of faith or grace.

If you want such a gospel, then, says the Lord, you have to be able to look after the whole creation, and you have to be able to fix all the world's problems and bring all the bad guys to justice too. If you can do all that, then, God says, you could save yourself.

This is divine hyperbole. It is the most sublime irony—everything the friends have said is turned around and aimed straight at them. You want to believe such a gospel—show me! Make it work! And do it before the visible presence of the glory of the Lord!

And Job melts and responds in awe and exhaustion (Job 42:5–6).

It is as if this great and fearful appearance of God has been coming toward Job, firing question after question and giving one and all the sense that Job was about to be severely punished for his pride and self-righteousness. Then, as the whole scene reaches a crescendo, Job, like a little child, cries out with an undifferentiated expression of sorrow and grief—perhaps expecting to die for reasons that still made no sense to him.

Then, at the moment when we expect God to take Job out, the whole movement of the glory cloud stops short, makes a sudden left turn, and sweeps down on the three friends—now God's anger and judgment arrive at their true destination. Job's cry is not acknowledged. Rather, as if escaping death by inches, Job looks up to hear the vindication he has craved all this time, and his past warnings to the friends (see Job 19:28–29) strike home.

Job believed in a gospel of grace. He took God at his word when God declared him to be righteous, and he never let go of that belief for a moment. Now God publicly, and on earth, declares that Job was right.

> After the Lord had said these things to Job, he said to Eliphaz the Temanite, "I am angry with you and your two friends, because you have not spoken of me what is right, as my servant Job has. So now take seven bulls and seven rams and go to my servant Job and sacrifice a burnt offering for yourselves. My servant Job will pray for you, and I will accept his prayer and not deal with you according to your folly. You have not spoken of me what is right, as my servant Job has." (Job 42:7–8)

What is the basis on which a man might claim to be right with God? Is it what I have done? Or is it what God has done for me?

Job put his trust in God's word of promise (Job 6:10). We today can put our trust in a promise kept in history and to which we have, in the New Testament documents, the testimony of many eyewitnesses (Acts 2:32; 1 Peter 5:1; 1 John 1:1–3; 4:14).

Our Kinsman-Redeemer has come in the flesh, died and paid for our sin, been raised from the dead, ascended to heaven, and from there has poured out on us his Holy Spirit. And we have his Word in writing, as Paul tells us:

> I am not ashamed of the gospel, because it is the power of God for the salvation of everyone who believes: first for the Jew, then for the Gentile. For in the gospel a righteousness from God is revealed, a righteousness that is by faith from first to last, just as it is written: "The righteous will live by faith." (Rom. 1:16–17)

It is an interesting exercise to read God's address to Job through a second time—only this time, imagine that his words are being addressed not to Job on his ash heap but to Jesus on his cross.

> God: "Where were you when I laid the earth's foundation?" (Job 38:4)

> Jesus: "Right there!" (Col. 1:16)

> God: "Have you ever given orders to the morning or shown the dawn its place?" (Job 38:12)

> Jesus: "Every single day!" (Heb. 1:1–4)

And this is our Kinsman-Redeemer, our Advocate and Mediator—and he speaks on our behalf from a throne within the glory cloud.

How will you answer the Lord when he addresses these questions to you?

167

FOR FURTHER REFLECTION

1. Read Psalm 8 and John 3:16 and think about what it is to be a child of God.
2. Read Ezekiel 1 and Exodus 40:24–28. Then think through the implications of Acts 2 again.
3. Reflect again on the questions God fired at Job as if they were aimed at Jesus—especially Job 40:12–14.
4. John Chapman recently asked an assembly of students this question: "If you should die and find yourself standing before the throne of God, and if he were to ask you why you should be permitted to enter heaven, what would your answer be?" Then he paused. "Your answer probably started with the word 'Because.' Now think. The next word you said identified the person in whom you have placed your faith and hope for eternal life. Was that word 'Jesus' or 'I'?"

PART FIVE

A TIME TO RECOVER

CHAPTER FOURTEEN

GRACE UPON GRACE (42:7-17)

At the end of a trial such as Job went through—and we are not told how long it lasted—what would be the first thing you would want to do? The time for suffering is over. There are no more arguments to endure. God has told the world that you were right and everyone else was wrong. How does it feel? What are you thinking as you look at your friends—as you remember their words? Remember when they told you your kids all died because they had done something to deserve it? That you had oppressed the poor and were a blasphemer and had been punished less than you deserved?

Job's experience is not unlike that of many Christians who have been imprisoned for their faith—and tortured. If we rewrote Job's story and adapted it to our Western values and culture, at this point in the story everyone would be receiving support and the play would close with all the cast being taken away for counseling. After the counselors would come the lawyers and the litigation. The talk-back radio would be running hot, and the tabloids would be getting rich as the masses express their outrage at Job's friends. A bank would sponsor a relief fund for Job as well. Is that how it should end?

God's priorities are interesting, aren't they? Watch:

After the LORD had said these things to Job, he said to Eliphaz the Temanite, "I am angry with you and your two friends, because you have not spoken of me what is right, as my servant Job has. So now take seven bulls and seven rams and go to my servant Job and sacrifice a burnt offering for yourselves. My servant Job will pray for you, and I will accept his prayer and not deal with you according to your folly. You have not spoken of me what is right, as my servant Job has." So Eliphaz the Temanite, Bildad the Shuhite and Zophar the Naamathite did what the LORD told them; and the LORD accepted Job's prayer. (Job 42:7–9)

After vindicating Job, God's first priority is to restore and forgive Job's friends and thus to restore the friendship Job had once had with these people. It says a lot, doesn't it? There is Jesus, naked, nailed to a cross, near the end of being tortured to death as his enemies mock him, and what does he say—"Father, forgive them" (Luke 23:34)—as they roll the dice for his clothes.

It is this Jesus who says to us: "And when you stand praying, if you hold anything against anyone, forgive him, so that your Father in heaven may forgive you your sins" (Mark 11:25).

Some years ago an elderly lady arrived with her luggage at the Church Missionary Society Summer School in Katoomba, about 100 kilometers west of Sydney. As she arrived, a young lady saw her difficulty and offered to help. The elderly lady was Kathy Diosy, a Hungarian Jew who had lost every man in her family in Hitler's death camps. The girl was Hanna Collison—a missionary to Kenya—whose father had been a soldier in Hitler's SS. As Kathy recounted her story later during the conference, Hanna had to face some terrible truths. Hanna had never met a Holocaust survivor before. The question had to

be asked, so she approached Kathy with the truth. Kel
Richards records Kathy's response:

> You are my sister in Christ and I love you. When
> I became a Christian I forgave everything that had
> ever happened to me or my family. You mustn't feel
> that way. We are together, we are sisters, there is
> no barrier between us.[1]

The Christian community can multiply such stories millions of times over.[2] Whether the forgiveness
comes fifty years after the event, or when a pastor such
as Kefa Sempangi prayed that God would forgive the
men whom Idi Amin had sent to shoot him as they
stood over him with weapons poised,[3] forgiveness is
an amazing thing.

Forgiveness in English has all sorts of moral connotations. In the Bible it is simply about letting go of something. The same word could be used to fire an arrow or
free a prisoner.

How can anyone let go of the horrors of the Holocaust,
the murder of a wife, the betrayal of a friend, being mocked
and abused in circumstances like Job's, or so many other
experiences occurring all around the world?

It starts when we stand at the foot of the cross and
see what it cost God to forgive *us*. When that concept hits
home, then forgiving others comes naturally. If God would
become a man in order to die for me, I can condemn no
one, nor can I cling to hate and dreams of vengeance. I am
too ashamed to be able to do that (Ezek. 16:63). Jesus said,
"He who has been forgiven little loves little" (Luke 7:47).
Then there is Jesus who committed no sin and loved more!

First priority for God and for Job is to get those friends
forgiven and restored. Grace is vindicated. Now it is time
to put it into action.

So Job, the suffering servant, becomes Job, the priest,
again. This time it is not for his children that he prays,

but for the friends who betrayed him. Imagine being one of those friends and handing your animals over to die in your place—to Job. Imagine being Job as you take out the knife to cut the throat of those fourteen animals. And then the fire—burning the carcasses of seven bulls and seven rams is no small thing. There but for the grace of God. . . . And that's the point. The gospel Job clung to through all of this was about God becoming a man and taking Job's place and paying for his sin, the friends' sins, and ours. It is overwhelming grace, and it answers all our questions.

AND SO TO THE PARTY

Enough of these tears. Bring on the food and the wine, and gather the family. Job is healed and restored, and the trials are over.

> After Job had prayed for his friends, the LORD made him prosperous again and gave him twice as much as he had before. All his brothers and sisters and everyone who had known him before came and ate with him in his house. They comforted and consoled him over all the trouble the LORD had brought upon him, and each one gave him a piece of silver and a gold ring. (Job 42:10–11)

It is significant that none of our questions are even noticed here. We wonder—where did all these brothers and sisters come from? Where were they when Job needed them? What's the idea of giving him silver and gold rings now that he is recovered? Or is this the family putting their hands in their pockets to give Job a new financial start?

It would appear that such questions have faded into the background as the celebrations begin. The focus is all on a joy released from a great amount of pressure.

It is interesting, though, to juxtapose the comfort and consolation that now are forthcoming with what has passed. Perhaps, until the Lord vindicated Job, such comfort and consolation were not possible. Wishful thinking and lovely sentimental words about a bright future are like salt on a raw wound when Job is on his ash heap calling on God to vindicate him. It's not about the money. It's not even about the kids. At the deepest level, the issue has been about life itself. What's the point? Is there a point? Where is the truth in all this mess? Wishful thinking and lovely sentimental expressions can be annoying at such times.

But now the questions have been answered, and everyone can join in and enjoy those answers. And there is comfort in being surrounded by people who are witnesses to the vindication of the gospel. It's nice to come home.

It is in the pattern of the New Testament's picture of our future that at the end of our struggle, when Jesus returns, the first item on the agenda is the party.

> "Let us rejoice and be glad
>   and give him glory!
> For the wedding of the Lamb has come,
>   and his bride has made herself ready.
> Fine linen, bright and clean,
>   was given her to wear."
> (Fine linen stands for the righteous acts of the saints.)
>
> Then the angel said to me, "Write: 'Blessed are those who are invited to the wedding supper of the Lamb!'" And he added, "These are the true words of God." (Rev. 19:7–9)

In hindsight, as we look back through the time of Jesus' public ministry, many of Jesus' actions and words suddenly make sense—but only after we know about his arrest, trial, crucifixion, resurrection, ascension, and the outpouring of the Holy Spirit at Pentecost.

Why did Jesus choose to take his disciples up a mountain and have them see the glory of the Lord and hear his voice and spend time with Elijah and Moses (Matt. 17:1–13; Mark 9:2–13; Luke 9:28–36)? How did this help them understand what was about to happen—except perhaps the cryptic clue that no one has ever found the bodies of Moses or Elijah either. God's words on the mountain are a repeat of what he had said earlier.

Why would Jesus spend the night of his betrayal telling his disciples that after he was gone they were to have a meal together regularly and remember what was about to happen (Matt. 26:17–30; Mark 14:12–26; Luke 22:7–23)?

It helps to keep our eyes on the future and to assure us of the truth of this gospel that ultimately will be vindicated when Jesus returns. How many brothers and sisters will turn up then whom we have never known? And what will be their stories—when all present will have walked where Job walked in their own way? At the Lord's Table, when the local church assembles and we pause to remember, look around, "discern the body of Christ [the people, not the bread]" (1 Cor. 11:29)—it gives cause to wonder.

A FORETASTE OF PARADISE

When God created man and woman, he told them to "be fruitful and increase in number; fill the earth and subdue it. Rule over the fish of the sea and the birds of the air and over every living creature that moves on the ground" (Gen. 1:28). Job certainly appears to fulfill this commission. The latter part of his life looks like as close to a return to Eden as would be seen in the Bible.

176

The LORD blessed the latter part of Job's life more than the first. He had fourteen thousand sheep, six thousand camels, a thousand yoke of oxen and a thousand donkeys. And he also had seven sons and three daughters. The first daughter he named Jemimah, the second Keziah and the third Keren-Happuch. Nowhere in all the land were there found women as beautiful as Job's daughters, and their father granted them an inheritance along with their brothers. After this, Job lived a hundred and forty years; he saw his children and their children to the fourth generation. And so he died, old and full of years. (Job 42:12–17)

In Job 42:10, we are told that Job got back double of everything he had lost, and the numbers are there to make clear that God did that literally.

It is hard to understand how justice and grace can exist side by side as attributes of God. The cross resolves that question as justice is done and grace is accomplished as a result. Here again we have the two together.

Job had rightly declared:

"Naked I came from my mother's womb,
    and naked I will depart.
The LORD gave and the LORD has taken away;
    may the name of the LORD be praised."
    (Job 1:21)

We have nothing of our own. All belongs to God, and he is within his rights to do with his workmanship whatever he wants (Rom. 9:20–21). This point has been made clearly by the questions God has just finished firing at Job. He owns the cattle on a thousand hills (Ps. 50:9–12). He owes Job nothing. And yet he gives Job double of everything that he lost, and in doing so God has fulfilled the law as later revealed to Moses concerning stolen, lost, or damaged property (Ex. 22:1–15). God gives to Job what Job would have had a right to recover from the Sabeans and Chaldeans (Job 1:13–17). Grace and justice here operate together because that is the character of God.

It is interesting that he also got double the number of children, although at first this seems not to be the case. Animals won't rise from the dead, but sons and daughters will. I must admit wondering about his wife, though. There is no mention of his wife in this chapter. Does she return? Did she ever leave? Who was the mother of these additional ten children? We are not told.

It is also significant that the author breaks with the wider biblical tradition and gives us the names of the daughters but not the sons. It may be that this author knew something of the special delight a father takes in his daughters and the way in which they were a comfort and a joy to Job. It is fitting that at the end of such a triumph of grace, the sons and heirs are, as it were, taken for granted, and special attention falls on those who would ordinarily not be noticed. Wherever there is grace, there must be the older brother of the parable of the prodigal son. Such sons are faithful and wonderful men and their father loves them—but they can afford for the spotlight to move to where grace is most clearly seen. The daughters ordinarily would not have inherited land. Their father's generosity reflects a cup that is truly spilling over.

But the last words are sad. Job dies. It is an interesting speculation that if he lived another 140 years after his loss, and God gave him double what he had lost, that he must have been seventy when Satan struck. An interesting speculation—but we are still left with a sad funeral. Mind you, it would have been a big one with four generations that started out with ten children. A lot for which to give thanks, but ultimately it isn't right, is it? We haven't arrived back in Eden yet.

And that is a significant lesson to take away from the book of Job. What we see here is not the end of the story. The best is yet to come.

Job had already accepted the possibility that he might die before being vindicated (Job 19:25–27). The friends were certain that no godly man could ever end up in the condition Job found himself. They said that if he would acknowledge his guilt and repent, he would be restored.

So Eliphaz argued,

"Blessed is the man whom God corrects;
    so do not despise the discipline of the
        Almighty. . . .
You will know that your children will be many,
    and your descendants like the grass of the
        earth.
You will come to the grave in full vigor,
    like sheaves gathered in season.
We have examined this, and it is true.
    So hear it and apply it to yourself."
        (Job 5:17, 25–27)

"Submit to God and be at peace with him;
    in this way prosperity will come to you. . . .
If you return to the Almighty, you will be
        restored." (22:21, 23)

And Bildad:

"Surely God does not reject a blameless man
    or strengthen the hands of evildoers.
He will yet fill your mouth with laughter
    and your lips with shouts of joy.
Your enemies will be clothed in shame,
    and the tents of the wicked will be no more."
        (Job 8:20–22)

179

And Zophar:

> "Yet if you devote your heart to him
>   and stretch out your hands to him,
> if you put away the sin that is in your hand
>   and allow no evil to dwell in your tent,
> then you will lift up your face without shame;
>   you will stand firm and without fear.
> You will surely forget your trouble,
>   recalling it only as waters gone by.
> Life will be brighter than noonday,
>   and darkness will become like morning."
>   (Job 11:13–17)

And here is Job, enjoying all the things they said he would enjoy—but he didn't turn and acknowledge his guilt or accept that all this suffering was a punishment from God for his sin. Quite the contrary! God has done all this as a vindication of his servant in the face of such accusations.

But now Job is dead.

And with him many other saints of God.

And so we look for the resurrection. We look beyond the ash heap and beyond the grave to the day when another Suffering Servant will return, raise his own from their graves, and bring us into a new creation—better than Eden. And that will be the ultimate vindication of the righteousness we have received by faith through Christ.

Till then, we live by persevering faith, and we cling to the words of the Holy One who tells us:

> Do you not know that the wicked will not inherit the kingdom of God? Do not be deceived: Neither the sexually immoral nor idolaters nor adulterers nor male prostitutes nor homosexual offenders nor thieves nor the greedy nor drunkards nor slanderers nor swindlers will inherit the kingdom of God.

And that is what some of you were. But you were washed, you were sanctified, you were justified in the name of the Lord Jesus Christ and by the Spirit of our God. (1 Cor. 6:9–11)

"My sheep listen to my voice; I know them, and they follow me. I give them eternal life, and they shall never perish; no one can snatch them out of my hand." (John 10:27–28)

FOR FURTHER REFLECTION

1. How would it feel to have been one of Job's three friends? What should they (we) do now?
2. How does Luke 7:47 work in you?
3. If all heaven rejoices when a sinner is converted, how should the local church respond? And when? What message does our response currently send?
4. As we sit at the Lord's Table and remember the price he paid, how do we also appropriately express the joy and wonder of having the right to be there and to eat and drink with the rest of his people?

CHAPTER FIFTEEN

REFLECTION: JOB, JESUS, AND ME

Maybe it's time to go for a walk and be alone with the Lord for an hour or two. If you have made it through the book of Job and these last fourteen chapters, there should be lots to think about. And maybe there are some serious questions we need to ask ourselves. I think of the scene in *Fiddler on the Roof* where Tevye has just been told that there is to be a pogrom in the village. He speaks to God much as if God were standing beside him. He reflects on the history of the Jews and all their suffering and wonders whether God would like to let some other nation be his chosen people for a while.

If you were Job at age twenty, and you could have read this book ahead of time—what would you do? Would you still set out to be a faithful and blameless servant of the living God, knowing that he would then select you to be the one to go through all of this suffering? It isn't a fair question—at least not for Job. But after what we have read in the rest of the Bible and seen particularly in the New Testament, it is a serious question we need to face. Maybe you would like to go to your quiet place and be alone with the Lord and pray and think this through.

When Jesus called his disciples he told them:

> "Whoever acknowledges me before men, I will also acknowledge him before my Father in heaven. But whoever disowns me before men, I will disown him before my Father in heaven. Do not suppose that I have come to bring peace to the earth. I did not come to bring peace, but a sword. For I have come to turn 'a man against his father, a daughter against her mother, a daughter-in-law against her mother-in-law—a man's enemies will be the members of his own household.' Anyone who loves his father or mother more than me is not worthy of me; anyone who loves his son or daughter more than me is not worthy of me; and anyone who does not take his cross and follow me is not worthy of me. Whoever finds his life will lose it, and whoever loses his life for my sake will find it." (Matt. 10:32–39)

> "If anyone would come after me, he must deny himself and take up his cross and follow me. For whoever wants to save his life will lose it, but whoever loses his life for me will find it." (Matt. 16:24–25)

Do you still want to be a Christian?

A Muslim student presents himself. He tells of visiting his relatives in Lebanon and seeing the guns and rocket launchers in the garage. His family have fled the country. The father tells you he wanted to give his children a choice and not have them forced into the cycle of blood feud and war that he had known. Now the young man wishes to become a Christian. But he is afraid to tell his parents, because if the relatives find out they will force his parents to send him back to Lebanon and make him return to Islam. He is genuinely afraid.

Would you, in his place, want to be a Christian? Would you encourage this young man to give his life to Christ and to acknowledge Jesus as his Lord to his family?

Every day, all over the world, people are making such choices and facing some frightful consequences. How many times have we dealt with women who come to faith in Christ but go home to face a violent and terrifying husband who will forbid them to have any contact with Christ's people—or worse?

There are so many ways in which the choice to follow Christ involves taking up a cross. At the simplest level, it involves continuing to live in a fallen world, with a body that is breaking down. It can mean all sorts of things along the spectrum.

It is worth taking some time to wonder at this reality. When we turn back in our Bibles to Genesis 3 and review the curses God imposed on the man and the woman as a consequence for their sin, we could ask ourselves what effect Jesus' sacrifice in our place has had. How many times are we told that if we repent and believe in him we will be declared righteous by God—washed, justified, and sanctified (1 Cor. 6:11)? If Jesus died to take away our sin and lift the curse, why do Christian women still experience the curse on pregnancy and childbirth? Why do our bodies still fall apart and end up being swallowed by the ground? And why do we still live in a world of injustice, suffering, and violence not unlike what we read about before the flood (Gen. 6:5)?

Let's reflect on the pattern that we see in the lives of Job, Jesus, and then ourselves!

1. It Is All Going According to Plan

Before God created the heavens and the earth, he had a plan, and in that plan were Job, Jesus, and you and me.

> In him we were also chosen, having been predes-
> tined according to the plan of him who works out
> everything in conformity with the purpose of his
> will. (Eph. 1:11)

Job was created to accomplish the things we have
been reading about. He was given the riches and the
children and the blessings for this purpose. His friends
were created by God to fulfill their part in the whole
experience as well. The outcome is never in doubt
for God. It is revealed progressively as each one lives
through the experience and wrestles through the choices
he has to make.

People argue over the issue of God's control and our
free will. That debate doesn't seem to be happening within
the Bible. It is a potential question addressed by Paul in
Romans 9, but no one seems to be arguing against either
the sovereignty of God or the integrity of human choices.
What for us may be a difficult concept to grasp with our
minds is a living reality that we know every minute of
every day.

In 1971, I went camping with some friends over the
Easter weekend. On the Saturday night the guys were
bored, and they decided we should go rabbit shooting.
Because I was the only one with a rifle, I got to do the
shooting. So off we went down the back roads looking for
bunnies.

No bunnies (which would almost count as a miracle
in that part of the country). An hour later, the guys were
getting restless. Then, in the lights of the motorbike, we
spotted a reflection about 25 yards ahead that looked like
the reflection of an animal's eye.

"Have a shot, Jacko, flush him out!"

There were about a dozen of us, and everyone wanted
me to shoot that rifle at something—anything! So I put the
magazine in, slipped a round into the chamber, put the
safety on, and walked a few yards forward to take aim. As

I put the rifle to my shoulder, I was feeling uneasy. "What if it's a cow?" I said to myself. I took aim and tried hard to see what it was, without success. Then I started arguing with myself. I was trained not to aim at anything unless I could identify my target. I put the safety catch back on.

"What are you waiting for, Jacko? Shoot it before it gets away!"

The guys were definitely not happy and wanting me to end their boredom. I took the safety catch off, took aim, and said to myself "So I shoot a rock?" But I was still uncomfortable. Then, as the guys were hissing and urging me on, I took up the pressure on the trigger—

"No! I want a better look!"

Finger off the trigger—safety on—weapon down—back on the bike—move up fifteen yards.

We all gasped. It was a station wagon parked off the side of the road. The reflection was coming from the rear window right behind the head of the driver, who was slumped over the wheel, sound asleep. At that distance I would not have missed putting a bullet through this guy's brain. My first thought was "Thank you, Lord!" I stood in the middle of the road trembling with the adrenaline shock of what had just nearly happened.

Can you begin to imagine how that extra eighth of an inch of movement of my right index finger would have changed my life, let alone his? I was twenty years old. The horror was I knew how close I had come. I knew I could have chosen to fire. What I don't know is how God stopped me—but I do know that it was not his plan for me to shoot that guy but for me to learn some big lessons and to go on working out his plans for my life.

God is sovereign, and everything happens according to his plan. Our choices are free in the sense of being unforced and fully ours. But the one who created us does not need to violate that integrity for his plans and purposes to prevail—and I am in awe of him.

When Jesus came into the world, his life was planned from before the creation too. Jesus knew he was the Christ of Psalm 2, the Son of God of 2 Samuel 7, the Son of Man of Daniel 7, and the Suffering Servant of Isaiah 52–53. How many times did he explain this to his disciples and they didn't understand (Mark 8:31; 9:12, 31–32; 10:33–34)! When Peter stood up to preach to the crowd on the day of Pentecost, seven weeks after Jesus' resurrection, he told them that Jesus died according to "God's set purpose" and that "you, with the help of wicked men, put him to death by nailing him to the cross" (Acts 2:23).

Paul tells us that "we are God's workmanship, created in Christ Jesus to do good works, which God prepared in advance for us to do" (Eph. 2:10).

Unlike Jesus, we have not stood in the heavenly court or seen God's plans in advance. We were not there before the foundation of the earth. But we know that he was, and that his plans for us are for the good of all who believe in him (Rom. 8:28) and, ultimately, for his glory (Rom. 8:17–18; 1 Cor. 10:31; 2 Cor. 4:17):

> In him we were also chosen, having been predestined according to the plan of him who works out everything in conformity with the purpose of his will, in order that we, who were the first to hope in Christ, might be for the praise of his glory. (Eph. 1:11–12)

2. *It's About the Integrity of Saving Faith*

Saving faith is persevering faith. "For everyone born of God overcomes the world. This is the victory that has overcome the world, even our faith" (1 John 5:4).

3. *It's About Clinging to God's Testimony Concerning Us in the Face of Temptation*

188

That means overcoming temptation. It means not giving in to the world or accepting the accusations of those who would have us earn our salvation.

No temptation has seized you except what is common to man. And God is faithful; he will not let you be tempted beyond what you can bear. But when you are tempted, he will also provide a way out so that you can stand up under it. (1 Cor. 10:13)

God declared Job to be blameless (Job 1:8). He spoke of Jesus as his Son with whom he was well pleased (Matt. 3:17; 17:5; Isa. 42:1). And before all of heaven he declares righteous and holy everyone who repents and believes in Jesus. We have his word on that. And that word is our hope for eternity.

No, in all these things we are more than conquerors through him who loved us. For I am convinced that neither death nor life, neither angels nor demons, neither the present nor the future, nor any powers, neither height nor depth, nor anything else in all creation, will be able to separate us from the love of God that is in Christ Jesus our Lord. (Rom. 8:37–39)

4. It's About Having an Advocate in Heaven

Job, like us, needed someone to present his case before the throne of God and plead for vindication—an Advocate and a Mediator. Jesus, having paid for our sins with his own sinless life on the cross, ascended and was seated at God's right hand, and there appears as our representative head and our Advocate (Acts 1:9; Rev. 12:5). Satan's case against us has been thrown out of court along with Satan and his angels (Luke 10:18; Rev. 12:7–9). Legally speaking, we have already been vindicated and are being vindicated every moment that Jesus sits on that throne. And no one can go up into the heavens and change that. What for Job was a logical necessity that he believed must be true, for us is a living reality resulting from an act in history, as Stephen saw even as he too died at the hands of wicked men (Acts 7:54–56).

Even if we do sin and by doing so contradict our faith, Jesus has paid for that too, and so John tells us, "My dear children, I write this to you so that you will not sin. But if anybody does sin, we have one who speaks to the Father in our defense—Jesus Christ, the Righteous One" (1 John 2:1).

5. It's About Enduring Physical Suffering

The physical aspects of the sufferings of Job and Jesus may be the most dramatic and striking aspects of their lives from our perspective. It prepares us for our physical trials and warns us that being in the world, in the flesh, means that we will not be spared such things (Dan. 7:21–22; Rev. 13:7). And so we come to focus on the hope of the resurrection and the restoration of our bodies. And how we long for that to happen (Rev. 6:10)!

6. It's About Betrayal and Abuse

As Job sits alone on his ash heap and Jesus cries alone from the cross, we know we will have such times when all who surround us will mock or accuse us. To follow Christ is to walk against the direction of the society into which we were born, and that will involve offending and being offended by people we love dearly. For Job, it was wife and friends. For Jesus, it was his brothers, one of the twelve, the elders and rulers of the remnant of Israel—and even the crowds who once supported him.

7. It's About Being Wise in Responding to Our Adversaries

Job engages in a long debate. Jesus taught in parables and kept his enemies confused. Before the judges who tried him, he was silent. We too are called on to speak wisely and yet boldly of the gospel and to be prepared to own it and defend it at all times, and to do that without giving the enemy any grounds for accusation (1 Peter).

8. It's About Pouring Out Our Hearts to the Father

The emotional intensity of Job and of Jesus tells us that being a Christian is not a matter of Stoic endurance. Our emotions are to be tuned to God's such that when he laughs, we laugh; when he weeps, we weep; and when he rages, we are allowed to rage too. Imaging God is not just a physical thing—we are to tune our thoughts and our emotions in to his and then express these feelings to him in prayer without concern for dignity or ritual, as children sitting on the Father's knee, clinging to him for all we are worth.

> Cast all your anxiety on him because he cares for you. Be self-controlled and alert. Your enemy the devil prowls around like a roaring lion looking for someone to devour. (1 Peter 5:7–8)

9. It's About Knowing That Ultimately Justice Will be Done

Whatever we lose, we get back and more so—for Job it was double. Jesus obtained as his inheritance all of the people who would be saved and the kingdom that Adam had lost. All sin is punished. All injustices are put right. And so we can afford to wait till that day when the Judge of all the earth will return and bring everything before his court.

> And everyone who has left houses or brothers or sisters or father or mother or children or fields for my sake will receive a hundred times as much and will inherit eternal life. (Matt. 19:29)

10. And It's Worth It

But there is something else that we need to think about.

At the very worst of times we might wonder and wish that Jesus would come quickly and end the suffering and the injustice and bring in this glorious new creation. The writer of Revelation, the apostle John, from his place of exile on the island of Patmos, wrote to the suffering churches of that time. He pictured the spirits of believers who had been killed for their faith. They are seated among the ashes of the altar in heaven. They have been offered up, as it were, as whole burnt offerings. And from their ash heap

> They called out in a loud voice, "How long, Sovereign Lord, holy and true, until you judge the inhabitants of the earth and avenge our blood?" (Rev. 6:10)

At the end of his book he writes "Amen. Come, Lord Jesus" (Rev. 22:20). But do we really want Jesus to come today?

Every believer is torn in two directions, as was the apostle Paul (Phil. 1:23–24). On the one hand we long for glory—for the resurrection and the new creation and to be restored to the ones we love and miss. But on the other hand . . .

Who do you know and love who today does not know Christ? If Jesus were to return today and end the suffering, that would be the end of the opportunity for so many people to hear the gospel and be saved. Let us pause for a moment. Our families? Parents? Children? Grandchildren? Brothers or sisters?

Some years ago I sat with a godly older saint who had been a lecturer at Moore Theological College in Sydney, and we chatted about how we had come to know the Lord. He was a man acquainted with suffering and the challenges Job had faced. He told me that when he became a Christian, he wrote a letter to his grandfather in England whom he knew was a believer and whom he had never met. His grandfather wrote back immediately, obviously overjoyed, and he told Bruce that he had been praying daily for his conversion since he heard the news that his mother was pregnant!

Some years ago my wife went to Vancouver to attend a family reunion. Some two hundred people assembled at Trinity Western University—all descendants of Pat's great-grandfather. At that reunion, a man in his forties arrived who knew no one. He had become a Christian and through various coincidences had discovered that he had some Christian relatives and that they were having a reunion. So here he was. And of course, at the reception area, everyone had to have a nametag, which identified which branch of the family they belonged to. Having worked all that out, he was then introduced to his grandfather for the first time. Long before Donald was born, his father had walked out on the family and set his face as far from the gospel as he could go. Now here was his father's father and the grandson who had come to Christ in spite of all—what a family reunion it was!

We learn in the New Testament that we are "the body of Christ," and Paul tells us:

> Now I rejoice in what was suffered for you, and I fill up in my flesh what is still lacking in regard to Christ's afflictions, for the sake of his body, which is the church. (Col. 1:24)

"What on earth could be lacking in Christ's sufferings?" we might ask. Certainly nothing further would be needed to atone for our sin. That, we are assured, is finished. No. Every believer lives in and suffers with a fallen world, and by doing so we buy time for others to come to Christ.

The job isn't finished. More need to hear before that final day comes. For that to happen, this fallen world must continue in its fallenness. Our bodies must continue to break down until we are in our graves. Wars and famines, crimes and persecutions must continue because the only way to stop them is to bring on judgment day and end the time when sinners can be saved.

That's why Christians suffer. Job did. Jesus did. And his body, the church, continues to suffer, in and along with all of sinful humanity—so that others might have the opportunity to hear, repent, and be saved.

> The Lord is not slow in keeping his promise, as some understand slowness. He is patient [literally, "long-suffering"] with you, not wanting anyone to perish, but everyone to come to repentance. (2 Peter 3:9)

And that's why it's worth it!

FOR FURTHER REFLECTION

1. How does Matthew 16:24–25 work in your life?
2. Look back and recall how, through your past choices, you can see the plan of God unfold. How does that help you to understand the sovereignty of God? How does it help you deal with the present and face the future?
3. Habakkuk prophesied just before the overthrow of Jerusalem by the Babylonian army (2 Kings 24–25; Lamentations). How would the book of Job have helped Habakkuk and the faithful to face that trauma? How does that help us understand saving faith in Habakkuk 2:4?

4. How does the fact that, in Christ, we have been sanctified and justified help us to deal with the sinful choices we still make?

5. Make a list and pray for the conversion of those closest to you daily. Let the realities of a suffering world give urgency to your prayers.

JOB'S RIGHTEOUSNESS

Probably the most difficult concept in the Scriptures is that of God's grace. Because we are made in the image of God, the concept of justice is deeply ingrained in our nature. At a profoundly fundamental level we know, and we have a strong emotional commitment to, the concept that good works deserve a reward and wicked or evil deeds deserve retributive punishment. Even the highly developed and nuanced arguments of our western, secular, post-everything world have not erased this passion for justice from our psyche.

So when we read of some ancient patriarch, that God had judged him to be "a righteous man, blameless in his time" (Gen. 6:9), or "a blameless and upright man, fearing God and turning away from evil" (Job 1:8), our default understanding is that these were men who lived perfectly righteous lives from birth. But then we remind ourselves that all are born in sin, born the damaged enemies of God as a result of Adam's fall (Gen. 6:5; Rom. 3:23; 5:12–21; etc.). Perhaps then these righteous patriarchs had lived lives that were so outstandingly godly, compared with everyone else, that they had earned God's approval and were no longer regarded as sinners. But then, how would that fit with what the rest of the Scriptures say about salvation by works? How does "justification by faith" work with the ancient patriarchs such as Noah, Abraham, and Job?

At this point we become very aware of the difficulties we would have in reading back into the thinking of the patriarchs the New Testament's extensive explanation of concepts such as "substitutionary atonement" or "justification by faith." There is no indication in the book of Job of any prior knowledge of the history of redemption as set out in the rest of the Bible, except for the single reference to Adam in Job 31:33 (cf. Gen. 3:10) and perhaps Job 31:40 (cf. Gen. 3:17–18; 4:11–12).

This impression is reinforced by the extent to which the book of Job places such an emphasis on Job's pious lifestyle and wisdom.

On the other hand, along with Job's friends, readers who are accustomed to a pious and respectful manner of prayer and conversation are shocked by the unrestrained and confronting manner of Job's speeches, not only as addressed to the friends, but particularly as he speaks to or about God. In his speeches, the early figure who evokes pathos and sympathy quickly becomes a challenging and offensive character expressing almost pure vinegar and no honey. Consequently, as he begins the long soliloquy in Job 27, it is easy for a pious and godly audience to come around to the position of the three friends, and declare Job to be a very wicked and impious man who has brought all this trouble on himself.

In order to sustain such an understanding, the reader then must go back and deal with chapters 1–2 and, in particular, the repeated affirmations of both God and the narrator that Job was, in fact, "a blameless and upright man." One way of accounting for this difficulty has been to assert, with no basis in external evidence at all, that the first two chapters of Job were tacked on to the original "folk story" in a rather clumsy and unsuccessful attempt to reinterpret the whole thing. On this understanding Job was a sinful man who was brought to repentance only by extensive and intensive argumentation and even divine intervention.

If, however, we take the concept of original sin seriously, our first issue would be to come to some understanding as to how God, and the narrator, could declare Job to be "a blameless and upright man" in the first place. Was this simply a relative evaluation? That is to say, was this only a statement about Job's lifestyle in comparison with other men? If so, the book would ignore the question of God's absolute standard of righteousness. Rather, the author would be confining himself to the question of theodicy, or how an exemplary person such as Job could be permitted by God to suffer such horrors. The problem, of course, with this solution is that the language used of Job in 1:8 is from the mouth of God himself. It is spoken in the formal setting of his heavenly courtroom, and bears striking similarities to the language used in Isaiah 42:1 and Matthew 3:17. It clearly is more than a relative evaluation of Job's lifestyle issued by his peers. This is God's evaluation of Job proclaimed from his throne in the heavens.

If Job then really was righteous, one other option would be not to worry about how salvation worked or what people needed to believe before the revelation of the Mosaic law. Rather, we could assume that these patriarchs, having virtually no information as to how salvation might work, simply trusted God to come up with a solution in his own good time. Thus, Job would have believed in God to fix things, with no real content to his understanding of that commitment. But then Job speaks of having put his faith in "the words of the Holy One" (Job 6:10).

Within the history of Jewish interpretation of the patriarchs, it is interesting to note the approach taken by the writer of the Book of Jubilees (dated to around 175–165 BC). This writer could not envisage any righteousness without the keeping of the Mosaic law. Further, believing in a God of absolute consistency and order, he concluded that the

Mosaic law had been enacted before creation. Therefore he describes in detail how the patriarchs observed the sacrifices, the feasts, and so forth, according to the correct calendar and regulations, and so were saved. This writer belonged to a sect even more extreme than the Pharisees. They believed that one's standing before God was a matter of being one of the "doers of Torah" (1QpHab 7:11; 8:1; 12:4; 4Q171 f1_10ii:14).

The New Testament also affirms that people were saved and received God's affirmation as to their righteousness during the patriarchal period. In Genesis we read of a few individuals who specifically were declared "righteous" or "blameless" by God himself, or who "walked with God." It is clear that others too were in favor with God as they received the covenant promises, and we find many instances where God's grace was extended during this period.

The writer of the epistle to the Hebrews is our most explicit guide as to how we are to understand the process by which the patriarchs were saved. Specifically we are told:

> Now faith is the assurance of *things* hoped for, the conviction of things not seen. For by it the men of old gained approval. (Heb. 11:1–2)

This simple statement tells us that when we find God declaring that a patriarch was "approved," it was through the patriarch's faith that this approval was given. The writer to the Hebrews goes on to tell us that that faith was not bare belief—an exercise in wishful thinking. Rather, we are told, its content was "Christ":

> By faith Moses, when he had grown up, refused to be called the son of Pharaoh's daughter, choosing rather to endure ill-treatment with the people of God

than to enjoy the passing pleasures of sin, *considering the reproach of Christ* greater riches than the treasures of Egypt; for he was looking to the reward. (Heb. 11:24–26, emphasis added)

But what did they know of "Christ"? The concept of the Messiah was one of many ways of understanding the person and work of Jesus. Each of these (the Son of Man, Suffering Servant, Seed of the woman, etc.) would be progressively revealed and explained over many centuries through many men and by a range of methods (Heb. 1:1–2).

We take Job 31:33, 40, as explicit support for our assumption that Job would have had some knowledge in some form of the events described in Genesis 1–11, at least. We also need to take seriously the fact that the book of Job is in the canon of Scripture and therefore is governed by that context. We conclude therefore that Job's righteousness had to have come about through his faith in God's promise of a Savior as expressed in Genesis 3:15 in whatever form and with whatever additional information Job may have been taught. Whatever he knew of the history of redemption, it would seem that Job was clinging specifically and explicitly to some promise or affirmation from God (Job 6:10). We have no record of God ever speaking to, or sending an angel to visit, Job prior to Job 38. So any "words of the Holy One" that he was determined to believe, in spite of all arguments to the contrary, must have been some form of the first gospel promise as it had come down to him. His faith had content ("words") and was not just "whistling in the dark" wishful thinking. Somewhere along the line he had been convinced that God had spoken a promise of grace, and that he could stand on those words with full assurance. We take it as a promise of grace, not works, because elsewhere Job is quite clear that he was a sinner and that God had forgiven him. The friends deny that he had been forgiven. And on occasion Job presents their case to God and asks God to speak to the matter. But he does not claim that he had never sinned (Job 7:21).

Therefore the book of Job is understood to be about a man who, with Abraham and Noah and many others, was justified by faith in the promise of the gospel. As such he speaks loudly to us today who may be justified by faith, whose faith has, as its content, the whole canon of Scripture and the written testimony of the eyewitnesses who saw God keep the promises Job refused to deny.

APPENDIX B

SATAN

As we open the book of Job and start reading it comes as a bit of a shock to find Satan in heaven. Almost universally, as we open the book of Job in churches and classrooms, we find the belief that Satan was an angel in heaven who tried some sort of coup against God and was thrown down to earth, some time before he entered the garden of Eden to tempt Adam and Eve. There is a substantial gap between the considerable amount of information about Satan that people generally think is in the Bible and the very little that is actually there. Satan probably appears only in three places in the Old Testament—Genesis 3 (and we don't find out for sure that it is Satan until Rev. 12:9), Job 1–2, and Zechariah 3:1–5.

Nowhere in the Old Testament is "Satan" a name, as it is in the New Testament. Rather it is a Hebrew common noun (or even a verb) and refers to an office or function. It means "to oppose." Most of the time that office or function is performed by humans. On one occasion it is performed by the Angel of the Lord!

It is always a good idea to try to work through information on important topics like this from the beginning of God's revelation and follow the way in which he revealed more and more information so that when we get to the

New Testament we can appreciate the significance of the things we learn there. Sometimes our knowledge of the New Testament allows us to assume that people in the Old Testament knew things when in fact they did not have that information.

Our understanding of Satan is also clouded by all the myths and stories that our culture has thrown up over the centuries as people who live in fear have used their imaginations to fill in the blanks in their knowledge of the spiritual realms of sin and evil. These myths and legends are, in the West at least, an interesting mix of biblical material and also of some old pagan superstitions and fears.

So we start with what we do know in the Old Testament.

The Hebrew word "satan" means an opponent, adversary, or enemy. In a legal setting it would refer to a prosecutor or accuser. Throughout the Old Testament we come across a range of adversaries or enemies.

When David was hiding from Saul he took refuge with the Philistines and operated for a while as something of a mercenary force. Eventually the Philistines were confronted with a difficult choice. War with Israel raised the question of David's loyalty. Should he and his forces march with the Philistines against his own people, Israel? Could he be trusted? One of the Philistine commanders, Achish, trusted David and wanted him to be included. The rest refused. And so we read:

> But the commanders of the Philistines were angry with him, and the commanders of the Philistines said to him, "Make the man go back, that he may return to his place where you have assigned him, and do not let him go down to battle with us, or in the battle he may become *an adversary* [emphasis added] to us. For with what could this man make himself acceptable to his lord? *Would it* not *be* with the heads of these men?" (1 Sam. 29:4)

Here the word "satan" is translated "an adversary." David would not kill an Israelite, and so they rightly suspected that he might turn and attack the Philistines. Here the word "satan" could also be translated "an enemy."

Similarly, in 2 Samuel 19:22 David had difficulty with Abishai and the sons of Zeruiah who opposed his decision to show mercy to Shimei. In response to their demand that Shimei be executed, David replied:

> "What have I to do with you, O sons of Zeruiah, that you should this day *be an adversary* to me? Should any man be put to death in Israel today? For do I not know that I am king over Israel today?" (2 Sam. 19:22)

Later, when Solomon came to the throne, he wrote to Hiram king of Tyre to tell him that God had blessed him with a time of peace:

> "But now the LORD my God has given me rest on every side; there is neither *adversary* nor misfortune [literally: evil]." (1 Kings 5:4)

Toward the end of his reign, however, as Solomon's faithlessness grew more extensive:

> Then the LORD raised up an *adversary* to Solomon, Hadad the Edomite; he was of the royal line in Edom. (1 Kings 11:14)

> God also raised up *another adversary* to him, Rezon the son of Eliada, who had fled from his lord Hadadezer king of Zobah. (1 Kings 11:23)

> So he was an *adversary* to Israel all the days of Solomon, along with the evil that Hadad *did*; and he abhorred Israel and reigned over Aram. (1 Kings 11:25)

These "satans" were the kings of the nations who fought against Solomon.

David wrote Psalm 109 as a cry against all those who had spoken lies and words of hatred against him. In a song that could as easily recall Job's experiences, David calls on God to help him and save him from all these men who have so many things to say against him. These men are "satans" to David—they are "accusers" who "speak evil" against his life (note the plural in verses 20, 29):

> Appoint a wicked man over him,
> And let an *accuser* stand at his right hand.
> > (Ps. 109:6)

> Let this be the reward of my *accusers* from the
> > LORD,
> And of those who speak evil against my soul.
> > (Ps. 109:20)

> Let my *accusers* be clothed with dishonor,
> And let them cover themselves with their own
> > shame as with a robe. (Ps. 109:29)

Probably the most interesting use of the word "satan" occurs in Numbers 22:22, 32, where God himself in the form of "the Angel of the LORD" operates as a "satan" to block the way of the false prophet Balaam. In this context the word means simply "an opponent." Balaam is here riding along on his donkey heading off to prophesy for the Moabites. First the Angel of the Lord, sword in hand, blocks the road before him. As the donkey then turns off into the vineyard beside the road, the Angel of the Lord again blocks his progress, this time between the vines so that there is no way around him. Here the Angel of the Lord stands as "a satan" or opponent to Balaam, thus:

> But God was angry because he was going, and the angel of the LORD took his stand in the way as *an adversary* against him. Now he was riding on his donkey and his two servants were with him. (Num. 22:22)

> The angel of the LORD said to him, "Why have you struck your donkey these three times? Behold, I have come out *as an adversary*, because your way was contrary to me." (Num. 22:32)

This passage helps us better understand Jesus' words to Peter in Matthew 16:23:

> But He turned and said to Peter, "Get behind Me, Satan! You are a stumbling block to Me; for you are not setting your mind on God's interests, but man's."

It is not Peter's place to block Jesus' path as he goes forward in obedience to the Father. It is not appropriate for any man to oppose God and his plans. Peter here is doing to Jesus what the Angel of the Lord did to Balaam. He is being "a satan" to the Lord.

Another interesting set of passages is the comparison of 2 Samuel 24:1 and 1 Chronicles 21:1. If we place the two passages together as they stand in the New American Standard Bible, we can see clearly the problem of reading the New Testament figure of Satan back into these texts:

> Now again *the anger of the LORD* burned against Israel, and it *incited David* against them to say, "Go, number Israel and Judah." (2 Sam. 24:1)

> Then *Satan* stood up against Israel and *moved David* to number Israel. (1 Chron. 21:1)

In 2 Samuel it is the LORD's anger against Israel that incites David to number Israel. "Numbering Israel" involves the imposition of compulsory service, either as a form of labor for the king (as Solomon and Rehoboam later required), or as here, military service. Under God's covenant with Israel, God fought the battles for Israel and they were won by faith, not by superior military force. Israel's army therefore was strictly a volunteer body. In setting up a form of compulsory military service, David was turning his back on the Lord and his promises. Comparing the two accounts in the NASB, the theological issue becomes, is Yahweh tempting or causing David to sin? In the Chronicler's account of the same incident "an adversary," unnamed and not identified, stands up to oppose David, and in response David calls for a census of his men. If we take 2 Samuel 24:1 as it stands, Israel has broken the covenant with the LORD in some way and God is angry with them. Among the consequences listed in the covenant curses (Lev. 26:17; Deut. 28:25) was the promise that God would bring against Israel as enemies the surrounding nations and Israel would be defeated in battle. So, having done this, God's actions against Israel provoke David to order compulsory military service. In the Chronicler's account, the Lord's actions against Israel are not mentioned. The Chronicler's interest is in the possibility of forgiveness and grace. Consistently he avoids going over and reminding Israel of their guilt. So here he simply states that "an enemy/a satan" rose up against Israel and, in response, David ordered the census. Here we are dealing with "a satan/an adversary or enemy" just as in the other passages above.

The word "satan" also occurs as a verb in these verses:

And those who repay evil for good,
They *oppose* me, because I follow what is good.
(Ps. 38:20)

Let *those who are adversaries* [Hebrew participle]
of my soul be ashamed *and* consumed;
Let them be covered with reproach and dishonor,
who seek to injure me. (Ps. 71:13)

In return for my love they act as my *accusers*;
But I am *in* prayer. (Ps. 109:4)

There are only two places in the Old Testament where
we come across a specific "satan," literally "the satan"—
Job 1–2 and Zechariah 3:1–5. In both of these passages we
are dealing with one specific "satan," who is not human,
and who is functioning as an accuser or prosecutor of God's
man. The satan in both of these passages is unnamed and
not identified. He is simply the one who holds that office.
In the light of later revelation we can be sure that "the
satan" in these two passages is "Satan" or "the Devil" as
we find him in the New Testament.

What is interesting, and perhaps a bit puzzling, is that
"the satan" as specified in these two texts is not introduced. Both writers assume we know who "the satan"
is. We wait till Revelation 12:9 to connect him to the
snake who tempted Eve and then Adam in Genesis 3,
but that connection then is certain. Essentially, at that
point, our information from the Old Testament, at least
in explicit terms, is complete. We have to wait till the
New Testament to put all the rest of the pieces of the
puzzle together—or as much of it as God is going to tell
us, which, it would seem, is a lot less than most of us
would like to know.

Complicating our understanding of Job then is the
common understanding that Isaiah 14:3–23 and Ezekiel
28:1–19 speak of Satan's fall into sin.

Against such an understanding we note:

In each case the text is a prophecy against the king of a
nation that has been an enemy of Israel—Isaiah 14:2–23 is
a "taunt" against the king of Babylon and Ezekiel 28:1–19

is part of a long prophecy against the king of Tyre. In both cases these prophecies are set amidst a series of similar prophecies against a fuller list of Israel's enemies including (Isa. 13–24) Babylon, Moab, Damascus, Ethiopia, Egypt, Tyre, and the whole earth, and (Ezek. 25-32) Ammon, Moab, Edom, Tyre, Sidon, Egypt, and Assyria.

In both passages the king's claims that he is a god are contrasted with the reality of his humanity—he is just a man like everyone else and he will be brought down to the grave where the maggots are waiting to eat his flesh (Isa. 14:11, 16, 20–22; Ezek. 28:2, 9–10, 17–18).

The language that attributes to these kings titles that claim godlike status are in keeping with the sorts of claims made by a range of kings and rulers, not only in the ancient Near East, but later by Alexander the Great and the emperors of Rome. Ascribing such titles here to these kings, and using these titles as "taunts," is an exercise in mockery and sarcasm—a judgment in keeping with their overthrow and the public dismissal of such claims as these men are brought down in military defeat and physical death. The description of Tyre as "Eden, the garden of God" and the king of Tyre as "the anointed cherub who covers guards . . . on the mountain of God" is in keeping with the location of Tyre (Gen. 2:10–14), as with the riches and glory of the fortress city of Tyre, the center of a trading empire based on shipping and navigation (see the references to sea trading in Ezek. 28:2, 4–5, 8, 16, 18). This city, set on an isthmus, was thought to be impregnable. Like Eden, no one could force entry into this city—not until Alexander the Great, that is.

Whatever words or passages in these prophecies that we might think sound like a reference to what we already know of Satan, the context makes it clear that this is not the author's intended meaning and that he is speaking of real human kings, not a non-human spiritual Satan. Tempting as it might be to allow these passages to fill up the gaps in our knowledge, to do so is to tear the text apart and use bits of it to speak of Satan and the rest to speak in its original context.

So, we do not know where Satan came from, but we do know that he was created by God and that God rules over and controls all that he does. We might feel the need to rush in and defend God from the charge that he, then, is responsible for evil and for the appearance and occurrence of sin in the world. This question is actually raised by the Bible authors and the answer is consistently the same—to whom would we expect God to be accountable for his actions? If God is to be charged with being responsible for evil, to whom is he responsible? This is evident, from God's interrogation of Job in Job 38–41 to Paul's discussion in Romans 9:20, "Who are you, O man, who answers back to God?" Rather we rejoice that the evil we see, and the suffering it produces, are not the remains of a battlefield after God and Satan have matched their powers, nor are they the meaningless and pointless phenomena of "nature." We rejoice that God rules, and that he works all things for his glory and that the God of all the earth will bring justice and peace through the redemptive work he accomplished when he entered into this suffering and took the punishment for our sin in our place.

APPENDIX C

DID JOB REPENT IN THE END?

Probably the most confusing and difficult issue in any reading of the book of Job are Job's final words in Job 42:6, which, in the NASB, reads:

Therefore I retract,
And I repent in dust and ashes.

Having read the opening narrative in Job 1–2, the reader expects Job to be vindicated at the end of the book, and indeed, if we skip over to 42:7–17, he certainly is. Along the way we struggle with the way Job sometimes speaks to and about the Lord in chapters 3–31. We are surprised if not shocked by the way the Lord speaks to Job in chapters 38–41, where he doesn't seem to be answering Job's questions at all. Then comes 42:6 and what appears to be some sort of retraction and admission of error on Job's part. This is even more confusing because God then, twice, proceeds to tell Eliphaz that, "My wrath is kindled against you and against your two friends, because you have not spoken of Me what is right as My servant Job has" (42:7, cf. v. 11).

We wonder then what Job has managed to get right. And what did he feel the need to retract and what sin had he committed for which he needed to repent? Our problems deepen when we turn to Job 42:6 and the text is silent on these things. Conservative evangelical scholars have traditionally made a distinction between the content of Job's arguments, which God affirmed as "right," and have allowed that Job here is retracting and repenting of the manner in which he has spoken to and about the Lord. The door then is open for every reader to determine Job's excesses according to his own tastes and concepts of godliness, prayer, and appropriate manner of speaking.

We can certainly find plenty of things that Job has said that would sound at least excessive or inappropriate on the lips of a believer. There is a significant contrast between, say, Job 7:17–21 and Psalm 51. We might sympathize with God when he asks Job, "Will you condemn Me that you may be justified?" (40:8). Certainly we might be excused for thinking that he did just that in 9:22–24. Surely, we might agree, Job went too far when he stated, "Know then that God has wronged me" in 19:6.

So, it would appear relatively easy to find things that Job ought to retract and for which he ought to repent. The problem is that God affirms that what Job said was right.

As we review the speeches and ponder these things, we notice that Job's words do, in fact, agree precisely with the Lord's. Thus Job can say, "He bruises me with a tempest and multiplies my wounds *without cause*" (Job 9:17); and God has said to Satan, "You incited Me against him to ruin him *without cause*" (2:3). According to the script of Job, Job had no way of knowing what had passed between the Lord and Satan in the heavenly court. Job has, out of the logical necessity of his faith in "the words of the Holy One," rightly concluded for himself what God had cast back against the account of Satan.

Obviously, this is a shocking and very dangerous concept. Has God in fact done something wrong? Did God admit to Satan that he had done something wrong to Job? If we had no knowledge of what had taken place in the heavenly court, we, with Job's friends, would easily conclude that Job was blaspheming. But at the beginning and at the end of the book, God himself makes this affirmation and vindicates Job for saying so. What was done to Job was *"without cause."*

In their rush to defend God from Job, the friends, and perhaps we the readers, have been so focused on that task that we have missed the point and stand, with Job's friends at the end, silenced, shaken, and certainly awed by the God with whom we are dealing.

If we turn then to God's speech to Job, we find, amid the long sections that assert the difference between Creator and creature, a small set of questions that sound like serious charges of error; thus, God asks him:

"Who is this that darkens counsel
By words without knowledge?
Now gird up your loins like a man,
And I will ask you, and you instruct Me!"
    (Job 38:2–3)

"Will the faultfinder contend with the Almighty?
Let him who reproves God answer it."
    (Job 40:2)

"Now gird up your loins like a man;
I will ask you, and you instruct Me.
Will you really annul My judgment?
Will you condemn Me that you may be justified?"
    (Job 40:7–8)

On closer examination we discover that these are, in fact, the very charges the friends had been leveling against Job throughout the debate.

Though Job has affirmed that God "reveals mysteries from the darkness and brings the deep darkness into light" (Job 12:22), Eliphaz accuses him of saying that God can see nothing "through the thick darkness" and that the clouds are "a hiding place for Him" (22:13–14). It is the friends who have exaggerated and distorted God's exalted place in the heavens so as to place him beyond any concern with earthly realities.

Job has consistently asked God to instruct him and answer his cries and questions (Job 10:2b; 13:22–23; 23:5) and he is the one who has argued that no one can instruct God (21:22). By contrast, Job says that one could learn everything his friends have said from a fish or a bird (12:7–8). Job, on the other hand, is full of questions, not answers. It is young Elihu who steps forth claiming to have all the answers (33:12, 33; 36:4).

Job does not find fault with God (cf. Job 10:3, 7). He is at great extremes clinging to the righteousness of both God and himself and seeking vindication of both (Job 27). It is the friends who find fault with Job. They claim that, if Job is stating that there is no cause for God to bring this suffering upon him, then this must constitute a charge of injustice against God (Job 8:3; 15:4, 13, 25).

Job certainly has wanted to "contend" with God and to bring his case before God's throne. Job wants God, not the friends, to hear his case and to decide between him and his adversary (Job 31:35). It is the friends who are attempting to contend with Job on God's behalf (13:8), and they are misrepresenting God (13:7). God's words to Job in 40:2 summarize Job's accusations against the friends in chapter 13.

As in Job 40:8, the question is whether Job is justified. Nowhere does Job argue that in order for him to be justified, God's judgments must be annulled, or that God is to be condemned for acting unjustly toward him. The friends, by contrast, depict God as entirely unconcerned with Job's righteousness (Job 22:3) and claim that human sinfulness is inherent in our nature as creatures (15:14; 25:4). Elihu has falsely accused Job of saying, "My righteousness is more than God's" (35:2).

God's charges against Job effectively summarize everything the friends have been saying about him throughout the debate. And yet God is about to declare that the friends have not spoken what is right, as Job had done.

We conclude, therefore, that God's speech is in fact a most confronting rebuke aimed not at Job, but rather at his friends. He has in awesome power appeared and put the question: "So who here is accusing me of wrong or trying to justify himself?" The dramatic redirection of these charges away from Job and onto the friends is a most powerful crescendo bringing us to the climax of Job 42:6.

Were Job to plead guilty to all these charges at this point and repent, it would completely overthrow the entire direction and purpose of the book thus far. What Job actually says is something quite different.

The verbs in Job 42:6 are difficult and can bear a number of meanings. The first verb, when used without a direct object, means something like "to melt" or "to dissolve"; thus in Job 7:5 Job's skin "runs" and in 7:16 he "waste[s] away." In Psalm 58:7 the psalmist says, "Let them *flow away* like water that runs off." Job repeatedly rehearses how he would respond were he to stand in the presence of God. He says that at just the thought of seeing God, "My heart faints within me!" So here, in Job 42:6, we might be better to understand Job's words as expressing something of that sense of overwhelming awe.

The second verb, translated "repent" in the NASB, has a sense of sorrow and grief, and can mean "to comfort oneself" or "to be comforted." Comfort, using this same word, is a major theme in the book of Job (2:11; 7:13; 16:2; 21:34; 29:25; and then in the near context, 42:11). Elsewhere in the Old Testament we read of Isaac being comforted after his mother's death (Gen. 24:67), Judah finding comfort after the death of his wife (Gen. 38:12), and David being comforted concerning Amnon's death (2 Sam. 13:39). The psalmist in Psalm 77:3 refuses to be comforted, as does

Rachel who, according to Jeremiah 31:15, would accept no comfort concerning her children (cf. also Ezek. 14:22; 32:31).

We conclude therefore that Job did not repent. Rather, the visible presence of the Lord, appearing at Job's request, brought comfort to Job. Job believed that this was the God who had given his word that Job was righteous and blameless before him. Such a response may be hard to believe, but then, if Job were wrong and these charges were right, there would be no salvation and no gospel and no hope at all. As the disciples said to Jesus, "Lord, to whom shall we go? You have words of eternal life" (John 6:68). And so with many other scholars we note the parallel with Job 19:27 and we translate Job 42:5–6:

JOB 19:27	JOB 42:5–6
Whom *I myself shall behold*, And *whom my eyes will see* and not another.	I have heard of You by the hearing of the ear; But *now my eye sees You*,
My heart faints within me!	*Therefore I melt/dissolve*, And I *am comforted* on [or *on account of*] the dust and ashes.

Such an understanding of the text is in keeping with what we find in the versions before the Vulgate, including the LXX and 11Q Targum Job.

The reference to "dust and ashes" may describe Job's location. In light of Genesis 18:27 (cf. Job 30:19), it seems more likely that it is a reference to his mortality.

At the end of the book, we are left to struggle with the realization that Job's suffering was, after all, "without cause." It is worth noting that the word translated "without cause" is an adverbial form of the same word that means "grace." Job's suffering was without cause, or *gratuitous*, because the ground or basis of his suffering was not to be found in him or anything he had done. Likewise, our salvation is *free*—a product of grace—because it, too, is not based in us, or in anything we have done. The scandal of a sinner saved by grace, and of a righteous man suffering gratuitously, is one and the same "stumbling block." We are not then dealing with an immoral God or an amoral God, but rather with the God of grace.

We don't need to rush to rescue God from misunderstanding. Job teaches us that it is better simply to cling to the gospel.

So, wherever we find ourselves, by faith, we climb on the Father's knee, and humbly look up in awe and wonder at the Creator of the world. We know that he is the one who extended to us his grace and mercy on a cross. We know he cannot be held to account by any creature, let alone by the objects of such grace. We know too that in his unfailing love, he hears us when we pour out our hearts to him.

PRESENTING JOB

The book of Job lends itself to a presentation in the form of a radio play or dramatic reading in parts. Given the length of the work, it often works to serialize the parts at appropriate places, such as in a series of sermons or studies. Where time is a factor, the book of Job also lends itself to a single abbreviated presentation by a careful selection of parts of each speech. The following is offered to assist in the preparation of such a presentation. While drama can be fun, it is important to keep an eye on the "fun." If done well, Job as a drama should have people arguing and getting involved in the substance of the issues, not distracted by the acting. Thus, it is important not to overdramatize.

DRAMATIS PERSONAE

(in order of appearance)

Narrator—A regular radio newsreader.
The LORD—A male voice from offstage.
The Satan—A cross between a lawyer and a spy.
    Think of a character who is a "James Bond," but

working on his own plans for the overthrow of the government that employs him.

Messengers 1, 2, 3—Men of any age over fourteen; men of the land who spend more time with cattle, donkeys, sheep, or camels than with people. The modern equivalent would be something between a dairy hand and a man who drives a large tractor, harvester, or other piece of farm machinery.

Job—A man in his fifties, quite distinguished and cultured, well educated, and of noble social class.

Job's wife—A noblewoman in her fifties.

Eliphaz—A gentleman of Job's age or older; a pietistic man, something along the lines of a Baptist deacon or church secretary, a Presbyterian elder, or an Anglican churchwarden. Most probably he would be a businessman or merchant, terrified of confrontation.

Bildad—Another gentleman, but more of a moralist. He wallows in the prospect of God's punishing the immoral.

Zophar—A clinical person. He is the logician. His theology is impersonal; he has no time for sentimentality. He is clinical and arrogant. The closest thing we have in our culture would be the stereotype of the cold medical practitioner who treats patients like "meat."

Elihu—A young man, probably a student, full of his own knowledge and righteous indignation. He is the "young Turk" with fire in his belly—out to proselytize the world and convinced that he is right and everyone else is an idiot.

FOR FURTHER READING

Andersen, Francis I. *Job: An Introduction and Commentary*. Tyndale Old Testament Commentaries. Leicester: Inter-Varsity Press, 1976.

Atkinson, David. *The Message of Job*. The Bible Speaks Today. Leicester: Inter-Varsity Press, 1991.

Clines, David J. A. *Job 1–20*. Word Biblical Commentary 17. Dallas: Word, 1989.

Dumbrell, William J. *The Faith of Israel: Its Expression in the Books of the Old Testament*. Leicester: Apollos, 1989.

Green, William Henry. *The Argument of the Book of Job Unfolded*. New York: Robert Carter and Bros., 1874. Reprint, Minneapolis: Klock & Klock, 1977.

Habel, Norman. *The Book of Job: A Commentary*. Old Testament Library. Philadelphia: Westminster Press, 1985.

Hartley, John E. *The Book of Job*. New International Commentary on the Old Testament. Grand Rapids: William B. Eerdmans Publishing Company, 1988.

Jackson, David R. "Did Job Repent?" In J. Azize et al., eds., *Uncovering Assumptions* (forthcoming festschrift for Noel K. Weeks).

Janzen, J. Gerald. *Job*. Interpretation (a Bible commentary for teaching and preaching). Atlanta: John Knox Press, 1985.

Kline, Meredith G. "Job." In *The Wycliffe Bible Commentary* (Chicago: Moody Press, 1962), 459–90.

Kuyper, Lester J. "The Repentance of Job," *Vetus Testamentum* 9 (1959): 91–94.

MacKenzie, Roderick A. F. "Purpose of the LORD Speeches in the Book of Job," *Biblica* 40 (1959): 435–45.

Moore, R. D. "The Integrity of Job," *Catholic Biblical Quarterly* 45 (1983): 17–31.

Morrow, William. "Consolation, Rejection, and Repentance in Job 42:6," *Journal of Biblical Literature* 105 (1986): 211–25.

Muenchow, Charles. "Dust and Dirt in Job 42:6," *Journal of Biblical Literature* 108 (1989): 597–611.

Newell, B. Lynn. "Job: Repentant or Rebellious?" *Westminster Theological Journal* 46 (1984): 298–316.

O'Connor, Daniel J. "Job's Final Word—'I am consoled ...' (42:6b)," *Irish Theological Quarterly* 50 (1983): 181–97.

Parunak, H. Van Dyke. "A Semantic Survey of NHM," *Biblica* 56 (1975): 520–21.

Patrick, Dale. "The Translation of Job XLII 6," *Vetus Testamentum* 26 (1976): 369–71.

Pope, Marvin H. *Job: Introduction, Translation, and Notes.* The Anchor Bible Commentary 15. Garden City: Doubleday & Company, 1973.

Rowley, H. H. *Job: New Century Bible.* Grand Rapids: William B. Eerdmans, 1970.

Scholnick, Sylvia Huberman. "The Meaning of Mispat in the Book of Job," *Journal of Biblical Literature* 101 (1982): 521–29.

Tilley, T. W. "God and the Silencing of Job," *Modern Theology* 5 (1989): 257–70.

Tsevat, Matitiahu. "The Meaning of the Book of Job," *Hebrew Union College Annual* 37 (1966): 73–106.

Williams, James G. "'You Have Not Spoken Truth of Me,'—Mystery and Irony in Job," *Zeitschrift für die alttestamentliche Wissenschaft* 83 (1971): 231–55.

Wilson, Lindsay. *Protest and Faith in the Book of Job: An Holistic Reading.* Unpublished ThM thesis, Australian College of Theology, 1991.

Wolfers, David. *Deep Things out of Darkness: The Book of Job.* Grand Rapids: Eerdmans, 1995.

Wolters, Al. "A Child of Dust and Ashes (Job 42:6b)," *Zeitschrift für die alttestamentliche Wissenschaft* 102 (1990): 116–19.

Zuckerman, Bruce. *Job the Silent: A Study in Historical Counterpoint.* New York: Oxford University Press, 1991.

NOTES

CHAPTER ONE: READING JOB

1 John E. Hartley, *The Book of Job*, The New International Commentary on the Old Testament (Grand Rapids: Eerdmans, 1988), 7, cites an Egyptian work dated to the twenty-first century BC that has a similar format to Job, including a prose narrative at the beginning and end, with nine speeches in between.

2 For a full treatment of this aspect of the book of Job, see Robert S. Fyall, *Now My Eyes Have Seen You: Images of Creation and Evil in the Book of Job*, New Studies in Biblical Theology, ed. D. A. Carson (Downers Grove, Ill.: InterVarsity Press, 2002).

3 See David J. A. Clines, *Job 1-20*, Word Biblical Commentary 17 (Dallas: Word, 1989), 10-11.

CHAPTER TWO: THE SCENE IN HEAVEN

1 Metallica, *Master of Puppets* (written by Ulrich, Burton, and Hammett; PolyGram, 1986).

2 See the discussion in Robert S. Fyall, *Now My Eyes Have Seen You: Images of Creation and Evil in the Book of Job*, New Studies in Biblical Theology, ed. D. A. Carson (Downers Grove, Ill.: InterVarsity Press, 2002).

CHAPTER THREE: THE QUESTION

1 John E. Hartley, *The Book of Job*, The New International Commentary on the Old Testament (Grand Rapids: Eerdmans, 1988), 73, and n. 12.

2 Francis I. Andersen, *Job: An Introduction and Commentary*, Tyndale Old Testament Commentaries (Leicester: Inter-Varsity Press, 1976), 85.

3 Most translations have it that Satan is saying that Job will "curse you to your face" (Job 1:11). The Hebrew word there, and at Job 1:11; 2:5, 9, is the usual word for "bless." The translations are really paraphrasing over the subtlety and the sarcasm of what is happening here. In Job 1:11 and Job 2:5 Satan is saying, "Reach out and touch all that Job has/touch his bone and his flesh and he will bless you to your face" in a tone that today would be followed by an aside, "Yeah, right! Like that's going to happen." In Job 2:9, Job's wife simply tells him to "bless God and die," which could reflect a mindset akin to euthanasia, as in, "There, there, dear. You have your integrity; now lie down, say your prayers, and die. You won't be in pain anymore," or it could be a vicious call to get it over with, as in, "So you have your integrity, and here you suffer. Put an end to it. Bless God for doing such wonderful things to you and die. That'll put an end to all your worries (and mine)."

CHAPTER FOUR: THE RESPONSE: WISDOM

1 John E. Hartley, *The Book of Job*, The New International Commentary on the Old Testament (Grand Rapids: Eerdmans, 1988), 77.

2 As told to the 1996 Katoomba Easter Convention. The video and audio recording of this presentation can be obtained from Katoomba Christian Convention, P.O. Box 672, Seven Hills. 2147 Australia.

3 See David J. A. Clines, *Job 1-20*, Word Biblical Commentary 17 (Dallas: Word, 1989), 61.

4 Ibid., 50.

CHAPTER FIVE: CRYING OUT AT THE SILENCE

1 See David J. A. Clines, *Job 1-20*, Word Biblical Commentary 17 (Dallas: Word, 1989), 64.

2 For the first term, *sha'ag*, as a verb, see also Ezek. 19:7; Zech. 11:3; as a noun, Judg. 14:5; Job 37:4; Ps. 22:14; 38:9; 74:4; 104:21; Isa. 5:29; Jer. 2:15; 25:30; 51:38; Ezek. 22:25; Hos. 11:10; Joel 4:16; Amos 1:2; 3:4, 8; Zeph. 3:3; and for the second term, *'anakhah*, see Ps. 31:10; Isa. 35:10; 51:11; Jer. 45:3.

3 See discussion in Leon Morris, *The Gospel According to John: The English Text with Introduction, Exposition, and Notes*, New International

Commentary on the New Testament (Grand Rapids: Eerdmans, 1971),
555-58; D. A. Carson, *The Gospel According to John*, The Pillar New
Testament Commentary (Grand Rapids: Eerdmans, 1991), 415-16.

4 See discussion in Clines, *Job 1-20*, 98.

CHAPTER SIX: CLINGING TO THE GOSPEL

1 We note in passing that the theologians [called "divines"] who
put together the Westminster Standards included a document they
called *The Sum of Saving Knowledge*. They were bothered by the
question as to what a person needed to know to be saved. Their
answer rewards a careful read.

2 See in this series Tremper Longman III, *Immanuel in Our Place*
(Phillipsburg, N.J.: P&R, 2001), 1-24.

3 Phillip Adams and William Lane Craig, 2002, *"Absolute Reality?"—
A Debate on the Existence and Relevance of God* (video CD, Sydney
University Evangelical Union, Box 58, Holme Building, Sydney
University, NSW Australia 2006).

4 See John M. Frame, *No Other God: A Response to Open Theism*
(Phillipsburg, N.J.: P&R, 2001).

CHAPTER SEVEN: THE LAST MAN STANDING

1 David J. A. Clines, *Job 1-20*, Word Biblical Commentary 17 (Dallas:
Word, 1989), 212.

CHAPTER THIRTEEN: AT LAST THE ANSWER

1 J. B. Phillips, *Your God Is Too* Small (London: Epworth, 1952).

2 For an interesting discussion of the issues, see William Lane Craig,
Time and Eternity: Exploring God's Relationship to Time (Wheaton,
Ill.: Crossway, 2001).

CHAPTER FOURTEEN: GRACE UPON GRACE

1 Kel Richards, *Forgiving Hitler: The Story of Kathy Diosy as told to
Kel Richards* (Sydney: Matthias Media, 2002), 191.

2 If you want to read more, may I recommend Philip Yancey, *What's
So Amazing About Grace* (Grand Rapids: Zondervan, 1997).

3 Kefa Sempangi, *Reign of Terror, Reign of Love* (Tring, Hertfordshire:
Lion, 1979); or the United States edition under the title *A Distant*

Grief: The Real Story Behind the Martyrdom of Christians in Uganda (Glendale, Calif.: Regal, 1979). Those men left before Kefa's prayer was ended, and later he learned of their conversion and the part they played in helping him and his family escape Uganda. Kefa has since served as a member of the Ugandan parliament and as a cabinet minister. Today he has resumed his position as founding head of The Africa Foundation, a Christian ministry to orphans in Uganda. Visit http://www.africa-foundation.org for more information.

INDEX OF SCRIPTURE